C000226601

Vivaldi

SUSAN ADAMS

To the members of the 'Red Priest'
Baroque group who inspired this
book: Piers Adams, Howard Beach,
Julia Bishop and Angela East.

A Vivaldi score, now held in the State Archive,
Bologna.

VIVALDI

Red Priest of Venice

LION

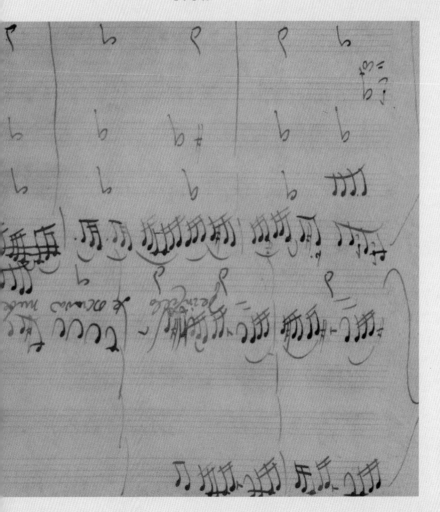

A Lion Book
an imprint of
Lion Hudson plc
Wilkinson House, Jordan Hill Road,
Oxford OX2 8DR, England
www.lionhudson.com

ISBN 978 0 7459 5353 3

Distributed by:
UK: Marston Book Services, PO Box 269, Abingdon, Oxon, OX14 4YN
USA: Trafalgar Square Publishing, 814 N. Franklin Street, Chicago, IL 60610
USA Christian Market: Kregel Publications, PO Box 2607, Grand Rapids, MI 49501

First edition 2010
10 9 8 7 6 5 4 3 2 1 0

A catalogue record for this book is available
from the British Library

Typeset in 10/14 Photina
Printed and bound in China

Contents

INTRODUCTION

The Molo Looking West with
The Doges' Palace, c. 1725,
by Giovanni Antonio Canal;
(Canaletto).

The stories of Vivaldi and of Venice are inextricably intertwined. To begin to understand Vivaldi as a person and as a musician, one needs to have some idea of the Venice into which he was born and where he spent the greater part of his life. And to understand Venice, one must delve back into history to discover something of her origins, her glory days, and her eventual decline.

In this book I have sketched a picture of the unique and fascinating Venetian Republic of the seventeenth and eighteenth centuries, in order to provide a background to the life of one of her more spectacular sons – Antonio Vivaldi. While there are numerous accounts of Venice through the centuries, there are very few contemporary details of the musician and composer whose home it was. In fact, the earliest biographies did not appear until some 200 years after Vivaldi's death. As a result, his life has necessarily been pieced together from records of his employment at the Pietà, the dates of publication of his compositions and performances of his works, and reports of his travels and appointments. There are references – not always entirely complimentary – to the "Red Priest" in accounts by people who did business with him, along with extracts from a number of his obsequious letters to members of the nobility. Not many of his words remain; however the longest extant correspondence, which covers the period of difficulty he experienced during his attempt to set up an operatic season in Ferrara, gives a fairly direct insight into the man – one in which, it has to be said, he displays his decidedly stubborn and impatient side, not to mention an uncanny ability to rub people up the wrong way. And yet despite his obvious failings in these respects, Antonio Vivaldi was able to inspire his pupils and delight his audiences; many of his instrumental works received rave reviews, and he was regarded by one and all as an outstanding virtuoso of the violin. Nowadays he is also without doubt regarded as one of the most influential composers of his age.

As well as throwing some not too technical light on the musical scene of Vivaldi's day for the benefit of non-musicians, I have at the same time attempted to reveal some of the more fascinating and bizarre aspects of the Republic of Venice that were influential upon, and formed the backdrop to, our hero's life. In view of the extraordinary resurgence of interest in the music of the seventeenth and early eighteenth centuries, this would seem to be an ideal time to discover more about the life and times of Antonio Vivaldi, mercurial genius of the Baroque.

PART 1 OVERTURE

Chapter 1
THE BIRTH OF VENICE

TAMING THE MARSHES

In the year AD 810, Pepin, son of Charlemagne and king of Italy, arrived in the northern Adriatic Sea, intent upon humbling the uppity Venetians. Having seized the island of Malamocco, the story goes, he asked an old woman – the only remaining inhabitant, the rest having fled – for directions through the lagoon to the central island of Rialto. "*Sempre diritto*," she is reputed to have announced: "Straight ahead." The deep-keeled Frankish boats, their captains unaware of the navigable channels whose markers had been thoughtfully removed by the wily Malamoccans, duly ran aground, whereupon the entire fleet was ambushed and destroyed by the Venetians. This legend, probably at least to some extent apocryphal, nevertheless throws a revealing spotlight on to the character of a people of extraordinary determination who, having created land out of the sea, were prepared to use the utmost cunning to retain it.

Venice is a city founded upon Alpine silt. For millennia the great rivers Po and Adige, and the smaller Brenta and Sile, deposited their sediment in the shallow waters of the Venetian lagoon, sheltered from the sea by the long, thin sandbar of the Lido. Over the years, the rock fragments washed down from the

King Pepin (d. 810), the son of Charlemagne, is depicted in this eleventh-century manuscript, *Codex Legum Longobardorum*.

Map of part of seventeenth-century Venice.

S. GIORGIO. M

THE BIRTH OF VENICE

mountains combined with sands brought in by the tides to form reedy mudbanks that slowly built up into marshy islets. At the same time, the river currents forged their way through the waist-high waters of the estuary, cutting deeper channels that snaked around the burgeoning islands.

The first inhabitants of this out-of-the-way area bordering the northern Adriatic were a scattering of settlers who began to trade the riches of the sea with the mainland. They built primitive houses of osiers and wattle and mud and perched them optimistically on stilts, while in their flat-bottomed boats they learned to scull their way through narrow passages among the marshes and out into the lagoon, the source of their livelihood. Without land suitable for crops or beasts, they worked either as fisherman or as salt-gatherers – both activities producing valuable trading commodities – and were reputed themselves to eat nothing but fish.

After the fall of the Roman Empire in the fifth century, waves of Goths, Huns, Alemmani, Lombards, and others seized the opportunity to fill the vacuum, each in turn fighting their way south on land-grabbing missions. To escape death at the hands of Atilla and the assorted barbarous hordes, many of the inhabitants of the mainland of the Veneto sought sanctuary in the strange, flat, watery marshes on their borders. The remoteness of these islands saved them from the attentions of the invaders, who had little in the way of boating skills and whose preference in any case was for marching on solid ground. As time passed more refugees, driven from their mainland homes, arrived bringing possessions and materials, tools, and skills that enabled them to start draining the marshes, digging ditches to create navigable channels, and building the first proper settlements. The wood they brought with them enabled them to construct permanent dwellings and, once they had acquired the basic necessities of life among the marshes, to build churches to serve their isolated communities. Unlike the pre-Christian Roman temples of the Italian peninsula, these early churches were built along Byzantine lines; they would be modified, if not completely rebuilt, more than once during the centuries. Much later, as wealth accumulated in the flat lands, new and grander versions of both houses and churches would be constructed of stone, the latter in due course decorated with marble and mosaics.

One of the most important activities of these early settlers was to develop the craft of boat-building. For it was their maritime activities above all others that would in due course bring the Venetians riches beyond their wildest dreams, turning this collection of small, damp island colonies into the glorious Republic of Venice.

The official date for the founding of Venice is 25 March 421 – the Feast of the Annunciation. Of particular relevance to a city that regarded itself as being under the protection of the Virgin Mary, this date was to act as the start of the Venetian New Year until the end of the Republic in 1797. A further time-based complication, and one that must have caused intense confusion to visitors, was the fact that the first hour of the day varied according to sunset and thus to season.

QUEEN OF THE ADRIATIC

Caught between the centre of Byzantine administration based in Ravenna and the advancing Carolingian empire in the West, the crafty Venetians managed to play the two powers off against each other. By 814 Venice had become independent from Charlemagne's Franks. While still officially under a loose form of obligation to Constantinople, she was free to devote herself to her maritime trading career. In a remarkable fit of generosity, the Byzantine emperor had granted Venetian traders freedom from dues and customs throughout his empire in return for their assistance in repelling the advance of the Normans, who had gained control of southern Italy and were aiming northwards up the Adriatic Sea. On this huge trading advantage, the fortunes of Venice would be made.

The island of Malamocco in the Venetian lagoon – scene of Pepin's debacle – became the base for the local Byzantine governor of Venice known as the doge (*dux* or duke). In the ninth century, the doge sensibly moved his seat to the island of Rivo Alto ("high ground"), which offered greater protection from the frequent inroads of the sea. Known in Venetian shorthand as the Rialto, this island rapidly became the centre of Venice. Canals were dug to channel the waters, and wooden bridges built over them. Thousands upon thousands of wooden poles were acquired from the pine forests on the mainland of the Veneto and driven side by side into the mud, to act as foundations for a city built upon water. Of equal importance to the future of Venice, the availability of trees of different varieties from the state-owned forests enabled a vast shipbuilding industry to take root.

Murano, one of a number of islands in the Venetian lagoon, became a centre of glassmaking.

By the twelfth century, thanks to the opportunism and enterprise of her citizens, not only had Venice become a highly successful trading post, but in the process of protecting her shipping fleet from the menace of marauding pirates she had also gained control over much of the western shore of the Adriatic Sea.

Unsurprisingly, the Byzantine emperor in the twelfth century, Manuel Comnenus, was less than enthusiastic about the power that had been acquired by his neighbour across the waters; in 1172, therefore, he determined to re-establish control over the eastern Mediterranean. His action in dispossessing, imprisoning, and even murdering the Venetian merchants and their families who had settled in Constantinople led to the despatch of a peace mission from Venice, headed by Doge Vitale Michiel. Among the emissaries was the patrician Enrico Dandolo, who was to return from this unsuccessful attempt at reconciliation having lost his sight. Whether he was partially or completely blinded, and whether by accident, design, or in a brawl – indeed, whether even in Constantinople or elsewhere – word went about that the blinding was on the orders of Comnenus. The Doge Michiel, on his return to Venice, was stabbed to death by a mob angered by his failure to win the day. Enrico Dandolo, however, despite his disability, became admired in Venice as a ruthless strategist and as a politician skilled in deceit – desirable qualities for the doge that he was to become in January 1193.

In 1202, the Franks amassed an army of Crusaders from all over Europe. Arriving in Venice, the army requested passage to Egypt, as an entry point to the Holy Land. The Venetians were able to provide the ships, but when it came to payment, the Crusaders were unable in their turn to stump

up the cash. The crafty Venetians, headed by Doge Enrico Dandolo, now well into his eighties, agreed to transport the men of this Fourth Crusade on condition that they first recaptured for Venice the Dalmatian city of Zara. This goal achieved, the city was sacked, the Franks and Venetians excommunicated by a pope shocked by their un-Christian behaviour, and the crusading army diverted to Constantinople. A revenge attack on

In this illuminated manuscipt dating
from c. 1460, Loyset Liedet (1420–79)
depicts the 1204 attack
on Constantinople during the
Fourth Crusade.

Coment la cite de Conftantinoble fu prinfe daffault

Constantinople had been part of Dandolo's secret stratagem all along: Venetian forces being insufficient for the task on their own, the fortuitous presence of the Crusaders' army enabled him to put his plan into action. Dandolo himself was to play an heroic part in the city's capture – this blind old man, standing fully armed on the prow of his ship, did not hesitate to rally the Venetians to the attack. Following the capture of Constantinople in 1204, the Venetians and Crusaders savagely sacked and plundered the city, the former removing as part of their booty the four famous bronze horses that were to adorn St Mark's Basilica – until carried off in their turn by that eighteenth-century plunderer of Venice, Napoleon Bonaparte.

The next 250 years saw Venice at the pinnacle of her powers. With a fleet of 3,300 ships she maintained her supremacy at sea, while through her trading activities she amassed vast wealth. She built palaces along the canals for her wealthy nobles and merchants; she attracted painters and sculptors, tourists and courtesans; she revelled in beauty and indulged in pleasure. Above all the arts, she delighted most in music.

SPRING

Chapter 2
EARLY YEARS

A VENETIAN CHILDHOOD

On 4 March 1678, the city of Venice was shaken by an earthquake. The same day saw an event that would shake the world of music: the birth of Antonio Lucio Vivaldi. Projected prematurely into the world, allegedly just seven months after the marriage of his parents, the baby was declared to be in *pericolo di morte* (danger of death) and was immediately baptized by the midwife. Showing an early glimpse of the determination that would characterize his life, Antonio survived this inauspicious start and was officially baptized two months later at the church of San Giovanni in Bragora, a stone's throw from the family's home. He was left, however, with what he referred to as a permanent "tightness in the chest" – probably bronchial asthma – an affliction that would dog him throughout his life.

Antonio was the first of six, possibly seven, children born to Giovanni Battista Vivaldi and his wife Camilla. Initially a barber by trade, Giovanni Battista was also a skilled violinist, who, a few years after the birth of his first child, became employed full time in the prestigious orchestra of the Basilica of St Mark. Here he played under the name of Giovanni Battista *Rossi*, no doubt on account of the colour of his hair – a gene that he passed on to his eldest son and which occasioned the nickname *il Prete Rosso* (the Red Priest) by which Antonio Vivaldi is still celebrated worldwide today. Red hair and pale complexions were not unusual in the Venetian Republic at the time, being a legacy of those early colonists who had fled to the Italian peninsula to escape the hordes of Teutonic invaders from the north.

The Vivaldis were far from rich, particularly as more babies arrived. The growing family was crowded into a small house in the *sestiere* (district)

This eighteenth-century engraving by Abbot Maffioletti shows the Venetian shipbuilding yard, the *Arsenale*, near to where Vivaldi lived with his family.

Giovanni Battista's position in St Mark's meant that music played an important part in the Vivaldi household...

of Castello near the *Arsenale* (Arsenal) – the vast shipbuilding yard whose wooden ships had been instrumental in bringing fabulous wealth to the Republic in its early days. Venice was divided into six *sestieri* – Cannaregio, Castello, and San Marco on the east side of the Grand Canal, and Dorsoduro, San Polo, and Santa Croce to the west. Each district was distinct and complete in itself, with its mazes of narrow *calli* (alleys) around the *campi* (squares), housing the tradesmen who provided the necessities of life – the bakers and butchers, the greengrocers, ironmongers, cloth merchants, and tavern-keepers, and the purveyors of every other household necessity. In fact, some Venetians rarely ventured beyond their own *sestiere*, having all they needed to hand, including water from the wells that, in view of the brackish seawater of the canals, formed part of the system that had been constructed to catch and hold rainwater. Wood from the mainland was also necessary for fires to provide warmth in winter when the myriad canals that wound their way through the island of the Rialto gave rise to a penetratingly raw and chilling damp.

In view of his poor health, it is unlikely that Antonio would have been able to join in the rough and tumble of a large family, so he probably escaped the daily chores that fell to the lot of his siblings. However, Giovanni Battista's position in St Mark's meant that music played an important part in the Vivaldi household, and this proved to be a field in which it soon became apparent that the frail eldest son could shine. His father, thankful that Antonio had survived his inauspicious introduction into the world, initially taught him to play both violin and harpsichord; it is likely that later he received lessons from the *primo maestro* or other experienced violinists at St Mark's. It is even reported that he played alongside his father in the orchestra at the age of ten, which, if true, indicates his very early talent.

Little is known of the rest of the Vivaldi children – Margarita, Cecilia, Bonaventura, Zanetta (Gianetta), Francesco, and Iseppo – other than that Francesco, who had followed his father into the trade of barber and wig-maker, was banished from Venice for five years for mocking a nobleman. It is also on record that Iseppo Vivaldi (a brother or possibly a cousin) was banished from Venice for ten years for having wounded a grocer's boy with a knife at two in the morning. The severity of these punishments clearly demonstrates the Venetian authorities' ability to crack down on rowdy behaviour.

THE RED PRIEST

Antonio's health problems meant that he was unable to follow a trade that demanded physical strength. However, it was not uncommon for a young man from a humble family to receive a good education by entering the church. Giovanni Battista (or Giambattista, as he was known in the Venetian dialect) and Camilla no doubt reckoned that such a career would improve their own social status as well as their son's, and would also ensure that he was looked after financially for life. And if there were any strings to be pulled, Giovanni's connection with St Mark's no doubt helped. At the age of fifteen, therefore, and without any particular vocation other than the urging of his parents, Antonio began his training for the priesthood. He received his tonsure in 1693, then passed through the minor stages of *ostario* (porter), *lettore* (exorcist), and *accolito* (acolyte), moving on through the higher orders to become a *diacone* (deacon) in 1700. During this time he

Giovanni Legrenzi (1629–90), Italian composer and organist of the Baroque era, who possibly taught the young Antonio Vivaldi.

lived at home rather than in a seminary, doubtless on account of his poor health. He gained experience by serving as an assistant to priests in nearby churches until finally ordained to the priesthood in 1703, at the age of twenty-five.

Throughout the ten long years of his priestly training, Antonio continued to pursue his passion for music, adding the study of composition to his increasing mastery of the violin. He was fortunate in that during his youth, Giovanni Legrenzi (1626–90), one of the foremost pioneers in Italian music and a Baroque composer of note, had been *maestro di cappella* at St Mark's. Legrenzi wrote trio sonatas, often for two melody instruments plus continuo, and composed church music and music for opera, his lively arias being based on popular songs and dance tunes. His influence on his pupils and on future generations, including Bach and Handel, was considerable. It has even been suggested that Vivaldi studied under Legrenzi, although as he was just twelve years old when Legrenzi died, this is perhaps unlikely. However, the young man would have had the opportunity, in the company of his father, of absorbing the techniques of the maestro merely by listening to performances of his works. He is also likely to have studied under Antonio Lotti (1667–1740), singer and organist at the basilica and a composer of opera and sacred music. Vivaldi's first officially recorded public performance as a violinist in St Mark's took place when he was eighteen and still in minor orders, although it is not known if he performed a solo on that occasion. Fortunately the combination of priest and violinist was generally considered acceptable in the Venice of his day: for a priest to play in an orchestra and even for an opera was not out of the ordinary.

Antonio Vivaldi has been dubbed a reluctant priest, for reasons that will become apparent. Certainly music was his preferred calling – playing the violin and harpsichord, composing concertos and, later, sacred works and opera. A year after his ordination, he declared himself unable to continue conducting mass due to the pains in his chest. Assuming that he suffered from asthmatic attacks or possibly some form of angina, it would indeed have been difficult for him to breathe easily or to project his voice around the church during services. However, it is also said that on one occasion he quit celebration of the mass, retiring to the sacristy in order to scribble down a fugue that had sprung into his mind, and returning later to complete his duties. For this misdemeanour he was reported to the Inquisition, which, regarding him as a musician and therefore undeniably a madman, gave him a surprisingly mild telling-off and formally relieved him of his clerical duties in future. Clearly it was realized, even then, that this impetuous young man would never make a conventional priest. It is thought that while he may have continued to say mass privately thereafter, in particular for his father, to whom he was very close, he no longer participated in the day-to-day activities of the church. But he retained the title of priest throughout his life, along with the nickname il Prete Rosso – a flamboyant alias appropriate not only to the colour of his hair but also to his fiery temperament.

Despite his apparent inability to continue his ministry in the church,

It is clear from all that we know about him that Antonio Vivaldi was highly creative, filled with enthusiasm, quick to act, and explosive in his mood changes.

Antonio Vivaldi was able to summon up a seemingly inexhaustible supply of energy for music. He developed into a virtuoso on the violin; he played and composed at incredible speed – in fact, he was positively hyperactive where anything to do with his passion was concerned. The question may be asked: did he exaggerate his health problems in order to follow his heart? Many years later in 1737, while attempting to resolve a business transaction, he wrote a whinging letter to his patron, the Marquis Guido Bentivoglio d'Aragona of Ferrara, seeking to justify the fact that he had not said mass for twenty-five years, and stating that this was "because of the illness that has afflicted me from birth and it oppresses me". He continued to explain that he had "said mass for a year or a little longer, then I gave it up, having been obliged to leave the altar three times without completing it, due to the same indisposition. For that reason," he continued, "I stay in the house almost all the time and only go out by gondola or carriage, for the pain in my chest or the narrowness of the chest prevents me from walking." This statement should perhaps be taken with just a pinch of salt, in view of the numerous travels in furtherance of his musical career that he did manage to undertake, despite his disability, throughout his adult life.

It is clear from all that we know about him that Antonio Vivaldi was highly creative, filled with enthusiasm, quick to act, and explosive in his mood changes. The fact that he was also argumentative, opinionated, given to justifying his actions, and unwilling to bow to authority were traits that would cause him difficulties throughout his life.

Chapter 3

THE OSPEDALI

CITY OF MUSIC

From the fifteenth to the eighteenth century, music flourished in Venice as nowhere else in Europe. Indeed, Nietzsche commented: "When I search for a word to replace that of Music, I can think only of Venice." For not only was music a vital accompaniment to the many religious ceremonies that took place year round in the churches that peppered the islands of the Republic; it was also celebrated in concerts both private and public, and in opera which, in the Baroque era, was a passion among the inhabitants of *La Serenissima*. So beautiful was Venice that she acquired numerous appellations: the Queen of the Adriatic, City of Water, City of Bridges, and City of Light. Nor was enjoyment of music confined to the upper classes; gondoliers sang their melodic barcarolles as they plied their trade on the canals, the verses often passing from one gondola to another. The gondolas were one of the sights of Venice: those owned by the nobles were painted black in order to prevent rivalry between patrician families; those belonging to ministers and foreign ambassadors were brilliantly and colourfully carved and decorated. The gondoliers themselves, dressed in their traditional costumes, many of them well versed in the works of famous poets such as Tasso, were known not only for their singing but also for their discretion, for they could be trusted not to betray members of the upper classes whom they ferried around on their amorous adventures. In 1745, English musicologist Dr Charles Burney commented that the canals were crowded at night with musical people, with "duets of music, French horns, and duet singers in every gondola". As well as the gondoliers, tradesmen sang as they went about their business; indeed, Venetians of all sorts played and sang spontaneously in the streets and squares. "The nation's enthusiasm for the art of music is

Canaletto's painting shows gondoliers on the *Canale di San Marco*.

incomprehensible," commented another visitor. Was it the calming effect of leisurely journeys along the canals and lagoon with the waters rippling against the boats that created a nation of musicians and music-lovers? Or was it pride in the extraordinary city that had grown out of the sea that made of the Venetians a unique people for whom music was a celebration as essential as the air they breathed?

Whatever the reason, Antonio Vivaldi had the good fortune to be born at a time when there was daily singing of sacred works in the churches and

A sculpture head stands above the doorway of the Incurabili Hospital in Venice, Italy. The hospital was designed by Antonia da Poute.

chapels, resulting in a never-ending demand for the supply of trained singers, as well as orchestral players to accompany them, and, of course, for composers to write new works. And it was in large part due to the genius of the Red Priest that Venice gained her reputation as a leader not only in vocal music but in orchestral music as well.

So where did these singers and orchestral players come from?

THE ORPHANS OF VENICE

Four *ospedali* had been built in Venice as early as the fourteenth century, in order to care for the sick and to provide a home for the many children who had been orphaned or abandoned through malnutrition, wars, epidemics – or illegitimacy. These foundations, variously described as hospitals, hospices, orphanages, or asylums, were originally intended for specific purposes and accommodated both adults and children. San Lazzaro dei Mendicanti is said to have housed mainly beggars, cripples, orphans, and widows. L'Ospedale degli Incurabili specifically treated syphilitics and those afflicted by incurable ailments. L'Ospedaletto cared for famine victims, as well as treating skin diseases and other illnesses. And the Santa Maria della Pietà is said to have taken in beggars and sufferers from ringworm, and in particular to have provided a home for orphaned and abandoned girls, including the daughters of courtesans – though these latter were said to produce few children, as "the best carpenters make the fewest chips". Such was the reputation of the *ospedali* that unwanted babies would be placed on a wheel in a niche provided for the purpose in the outer walls, in the knowledge that the wheel would be turned, the infants taken in, cared for, and often adopted by country folk. "Before the ospedali," Edward Wright wrote in the early eighteenth century, "bastards were thrown into the canals."

Initially founded by the church authorities, these charitable institutions gradually developed into *scuole* (schools) with a view to providing the abandoned children with a Christian education, as well as teaching them skills that would enable them to earn a living. It was not long, Venice being the city that it was, before music made its way into the *ospedali*, transforming them from mere schools into conservatoires. Youngsters of both sexes were admitted to three of the *ospedali* – though not to the Pietà, which accepted only girls. Boys from the other three foundations would leave as soon as they were old enough to be apprenticed to an appropriate trade. By contrast, the four *ospedali* of Naples – only one of which accepted girls – specialized in the training of boys and in particular the famous castrati. Naples and Venice, both dedicated to the training of young singers and instrumentalists, were to maintain a musical rivalry throughout the Baroque era.

Children generally entered an *ospedale* school between the ages of six and ten, though older girls were sometimes admitted if they showed

*Such was their musical skill, and
often their beauty, that these
young singers and instrumentalists
would become known to the public
as "stars" – a system of celebrity
existing in the entertainment world
even in those far-off days.*

particular musical ability; there was always stiff competition for the limited number of places available each year. Occasionally a few paying pupils would also enter an *ospedale* in order to perfect their music skills.

The most intelligent and gifted girls who showed some musical ability were selected for training, as singers or instrumentalists or both, becoming known as the *figlie di coro* (choirgirls). The less musically able – the *figlie di commun* (common or community girls) – were taught housekeeping skills such as laundering, as well as the domestic arts, notably lace-making and embroidery, at which many of them excelled. In the long term all the girls had three choices: to marry, to become nuns, or to remain in the *ospedale* for life, where they would either undertake domestic work or continue with their musical careers. In the latter case they would also be expected to look after and train the newcomers. Indeed, the *ospedali* relied on the older members of the *figlie di coro* who stayed on, sometimes for the whole of their lives, to act as *maestra* (teacher), for these women were able to contribute their considerable experience both to the orchestras and to the choirs.

Dowries of 300 ducats – a considerable sum – were provided for girls leaving to get married, though to qualify they would generally be required to have given up to ten years' service to the institution, and to have trained two or more students. Part of the deal on leaving an *ospedale* to marry was that these young women, these skilled singers and instrumentalists, were forbidden to carry on with a musical career. Their husbands were even expected to sign a document agreeing to this stricture, the reason being that it was considered unfair for a girl who had received a free training to go on to benefit financially from it. In fact, they were even discouraged from singing or playing in their own homes. The girls who were lucky enough to find husbands were

Cecilia, wife of the artist Gian Battista – or Giambattista – Tiepolo (1696–1770), is depicted as Rachel, in Tiepolo's *Rachel Holding the Idols*, c. 1726.

generally the most talented who had benefited from performing in private concerts at the homes of the nobles and rich merchants, sometimes far from Venice. Such was their musical skill, and often their beauty, that these young singers and instrumentalists would become known to the public as "stars" – a system of celebrity existing in the entertainment world even in those far-off days. It would have been from these contacts with the outside world (for there was little other opportunity) that some of the girls were chosen as wives by the young men and their families who had seen and heard them perform; a bride who had been sheltered from the world, who had received a Christian education, and who had attained a high standard in music was considered a highly desirable acquisition. Although to make a good marriage was regarded as the acme of success for the young women, nevertheless the girls must have found it hugely frustrating, after so many years of immersion in music, to be prevented from continuing to use their talents.

There is a romantic tale of one girl from the Ospedaletto who managed, against all the odds, to marry for love. Cecilia Guardi had been admitted to the *ospedale* at the age of fifteen, on account of the poverty of her mother and at the recommendation of the administrator of the Ospedaletto, Count Giovanelli. Her beautiful soprano voice soon gave her pride of place among the *figlie di coro*; it also brought her to the attention of Gian Battista Tiepolo, a young painter working in the church. Later to become one of the great Venetian artists, Tiepolo, with the support of his family, managed to abduct Cecilia and marry her secretly. This drama, which caused some concern regarding the dowry paid to the girl after her sojourn in the *ospedale* of just two years, resulted in a stiffening of the rules in this respect.

Life in an *ospedale* was generally austere and not dissimilar to the regime of a nunnery, concentrating as it did on the provision of a strict religious education. The girls who followed a musical path, being valuable commercial commodities, were lucky enough to receive better food and clothes than did the community girls, for it was important that they maintained good health in order to perform. In particular, it was vital to ensure that the singers avoided sore throats, and to this end these favoured pupils sometimes received the bonus of extra wood for fires in the winter. Doctors would also allow the girls the occasional luxury of short holidays in the countryside for health reasons.

In addition to the girls, both musical and community, there were many others living in Venice's *ospedali* – young boys before their apprenticeship, the sick and the old, and of course the staff. The population of each of the four foundations varied over the years, from around 200 to as many as 1,000, for example, in the heyday of the Pietà. The church paid for teaching only, the rest of the expenses being funded by the patricians – those members of the Venetian upper classes who had grown rich in the heyday of Venice's trade with the East. Furthermore, it was often the illegitimate children of these nobles and benefactors who, though not strictly speaking orphans, would frequently be tidied away into an *ospedale*, where they could receive a good education without bringing embarrassment upon their families.

This was the environment into which Antonio Vivaldi made his flamboyant entrance in the year of his ordination. He was appointed *maestro di violino* (violin teacher) at what was to become the most prestigious of the four *ospedali* – Santa Maria della Pietà. Situated on the Riva degli Schiavoni between the Arsenal and the Piazza San Marco (St Mark's Square), the Pietà was just a relatively short distance from the Vivaldi household. Imagine the effect of the arrival of the young black-clad priest (the wearing of the cassock being essential for males entering a closed establishment), with his flaming red curls, into this all-female establishment! The *figlie di coro*, a terminology that included both singers and instrumentalists, would have had very little contact with men of any kind during their lives in the *ospedale*, male teachers being kept to an absolute minimum. So the appearance of *il Prete Rosso* no doubt caused a surge of enthusiasm for their musical studies. As for Vivaldi himself, the appointment allowed him to maintain his status as a priest, at the same time providing him with an opportunity to forge ahead with what he was really dedicated to: a career in music.

The Piazza San Marco
(St Mark's Square) in
Venice. This painting by
Giovanni Antonio Canal
(1697–1768) – known as
Canaletto – depicts the
Doge's Palace and part of
St Mark's Basilica.

Chapter 4
LA PIETÀ

PRIEST AND MAESTRO

Vivaldi's first spell as *maestro di violino* at the Pietà lasted from 1703 – six months after his ordination – until 1709. There had always been musical competition between the *ospedali*, but such was the young priest's enthusiasm for his subject, his teaching skill, and his ability to fire up his pupils, that the reputation of the Pietà under his incumbency soon outshone that of all the others, both in choral and in instrumental performance.

At the time of Vivaldi's appointment, the *maestro di coro* (choirmaster) in overall charge of music at the *ospedale* was Francesco Gasparini (1668–1727), who was to go on to become a prolific composer of largely forgotten operas. Gasparini's remit at the Pietà included the writing of new works, overseeing the progress of the students, and masterminding the music to be performed in the chapel and at concerts given by the girls throughout the year. He was additionally responsible for selecting the best teachers of stringed instruments in particular, these being of the greatest importance in the development of the *ospedale*'s musical reputation. Despite the requirement to avoid male teachers where possible, Gasparini must have considered Vivaldi sufficiently outstanding to propose him to the governors; his choice clearly proved satisfactory, as shortly after his appointment the Red Priest added the teaching of the *viola inglese* to his tasks, for which his salary was increased from 60 to 100 ducats a year. Among his other duties he was placed in charge of buying instruments for the girls, in which capacity he was able to display his typically Venetian relish for driving a hard bargain.

Prior to Vivaldi's arrival, the Pietà, along with the other *ospedali*, was best known for its choral work. As there were no men in the choir at this all-female institution, it is thought that the girls with deeper voices took the lower parts; it may well have been with this requirement in mind that Vivaldi wrote more music for the baritone – a sound he particularly favoured – than for the bass. It has also been suggested that the bass parts may have been transposed an octave higher for the contralto voice.

Although the provision of new music at the Pietà was still officially the responsibility of Francesco Gasparini, Vivaldi soon found himself

composing works for the instrumentalists of the *figlie di coro*. This was greatly to the relief of the *maestro di coro*, allowing him time to concentrate on opera. Some of *il Prete Rosso*'s early compositions were simple and obviously designed as exercises for the younger pupils, but whereas the Pietà had previously concentrated on choral works, Vivaldi changed the emphasis by building up the instrumental side, and he was to write his most exuberant concertos for performance by the *figlie di coro*. For with this remarkably gifted group of singers and players at his disposal, Vivaldi had acquired nothing less than his own personal orchestra on which to hone his musical expertise.

The close contact between a male, even if a priest, and the young girls of the *ospedale* could have presented the governors with a problem. Reference – almost certainly apocryphal – suggests that there was no such problem in Vivaldi's case: Edward Wright states that the girls "have a eunuch for their master", probably lifting this from an earlier story that "a priest fitted for musick may exercise the priesthood as well as another, provided he hath his necessities, or if you will, his superfluities in his pocket" – "necessities" being testicles and "superfluities" indicating that such organs were superfluous for one bound to a life of celibacy. Bearing in mind that the Red Priest was later to be accused of taking a mistress, this comment must be regarded with a considerable degree of scepticism.

It was in order to broaden the repertoire of *the figlie di coro* of the Pietà and to cater for the diversity of their talents, which included proficiency on a wide variety of musical instruments, that Vivaldi wrote concertos that featured not only the more conventional instruments of the orchestra – predominantly strings – but also the more unusual ones for which the Pietà

Examples of the oboe
d'amore and a bassoon in
the Baroque style.

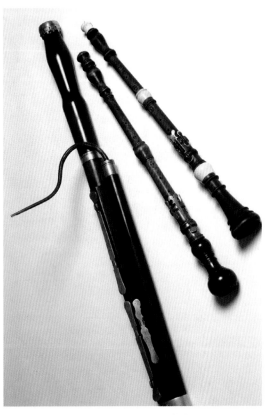

had become renowned. The emergence of the Baroque style, with its emphasis on spontaneity, strong emotions, and extreme contrasts, had created a need for instruments capable of a wider range of sound than had hitherto been available during the Renaissance. This was the period when Antonio Stradivarius (1644–1737), probably the most famous maker of violins and cellos that the world has seen, perfected the Cremonese violin. The Baroque violin differed in that it had no chin rest, the strings were of gut, and the bow was short and slightly convex, while the cello had no spike: originally known as the violoncello, it was initially used to provide the basso continuo, later becoming a solo instrument. As well as composing his numerous concertos for the violin and his twenty-five cello concertos, Vivaldi also wrote a number of works for plucked stringed instruments such as the lute and mandolin, including, for example, three concertos for a combination of lute, violin, and bass.

In the Baroque orchestra, the principal role of the harpsichord was that of a continuo instrument, sharing the bass line with the cello, although it was later to be favoured as a solo instrument in the great works of Bach, Handel, and Scarlatti. The harpsichord was also particularly popular among musicians in France. In addition to the strings and keyboard, the orchestra of the Pietà included woodwind players. The four major woodwind instruments of the Baroque – the *flauto* (recorder), *traverso* (flute), oboe, and bassoon – had all been developed and improved over time to the point where they played an important part in the sonatas and concertos of the High Baroque. The recorder and flute enjoyed a friendly rivalry throughout the era, and were largely interchangeable in Vivaldi's concertos – the exception being a set of four concertos specifically for recorder (one for treble and three for sopranino) that are renowned for their exceptional technical difficulty and represent the pinnacle of virtuoso wind writing in the Baroque. Both the oboe, successor to the shawm, and the bassoon, a development of the curtal, became popular in the mid-seventeenth century. Indeed, Vivaldi was rather surprisingly to write as many as thirty-nine concertos for the bassoon – this instrument presumably being a favourite among the *figlie di coro*.

While there were fewer brass players in the orchestra of the Pietà, the girls were competent enough to tackle the trumpet or trombone when necessary, usually in a supporting role to the cello. The trumpet, originally an instrument of war, was first scored by Monteverdi in his opera *Orfeo* in 1607 and later in that century played a regular part in the orchestra, being particularly favoured by Alessandro Scarlatti. The trombone, which had developed from the sackbut, was restricted in its early form to accompanying sacred music; it too was to play its part along with horns and kettledrums in church music whenever a military atmosphere was required, for example in Vivaldi's oratorio *Juditha triumphans* (see below). The early horn was used only on ceremonial occasions or in the hunting field; it was later to morph into the orchestral instrument known in England as the French horn, although it would not be until Mozart's day that it was sufficiently developed to take on a solo role. It is interesting to note, however, that French scholar and biographer Marc Pincherle goes so far as to suggest that Vivaldi may have heralded the introduction of horns into the symphonic orchestra.

The Red Priest, with his passion for the *stile moderno* (the modern style – of which more later) and his dramatic compositions, must have presented a very considerable challenge to his students, who nevertheless vied with one another to reach the highest standards of virtuosity. And clearly their efforts were successful, as we learn from the approving comments of the audiences who attended the weekly liturgical celebrations at the Pietà. Under Vivaldi's energetic direction, these events resembled nothing so much as a theatrical concert. Indeed, when an oratorio was being performed, libretti would be distributed to the visitors, naming the solo singers, causing them to become "objects of infatuation and intrigue". Visitors were not permitted to show their pleasure by applauding these musical offerings in church or chapel, for fear of turning them into secular concerts. It became the custom among audiences, therefore, to overcome this ban by shuffling their feet, blowing their noses, and coughing in the appropriate places instead. Vivaldi, as might be expected from one of his fiery character, was said to have a spirited style and dishevelled curls when conducting his gifted *figlie di coro* – bringing to mind, perhaps, one of the most celebrated of present-day British conductors, Sir Simon Rattle. Certainly the Red Priest's hard work and enthusiasm paid off; Charles de Brosses, President of the Dijon Parliament, who toured Italy in 1739 and 1740, was to comment that the standard of music at the Pietà rivalled that of St Mark's. High praise indeed!

As we have seen, music flowed through the veins of the Venetians like water through the canals of Venice. As a result, in Vivaldi's day there was a demand not only for plentiful music in the churches, but also for private concerts in the *palazzi* (palaces) of the nobles. The four *ospedali*, with their focus on training singers and players to a high standard, were in prime position to benefit from these demands. The elite of the girls – known as the *privileggiate* – were regarded as among the foremost musical performers in Italy, and a visit to a concert at one of the *ospedali* was high on the list of attractions, both for Venetians and for tourists from all over Europe on the Grand Tour. These musical performances also brought in much-needed funds for the foundations, the girls themselves receiving very little, if anything, in the way of payment.

The singers and instrumentalists performed behind grilles in the chapels of the *ospedali*, generally modestly dressed in white or black gowns, each girl with a thin veil covering her hair. Anonymity officially being the name of the game, the girls of the orchestra were usually known simply by their Christian names followed by their instrument of choice, for example Michieletta del Violin or Maria dal Cornetto. Unofficially, however, as we have seen, the stars tended to become known and celebrated by name. Audiences found their music enchanting and their half-concealed charms more than tantalizing. Indeed, Charles de Brosses praised the "transcendent music" of the establishments and commented that the girls "sing like angels and play the violin, the flute, the organ, the oboe, the cello, the bassoon; in short there is no instrument, however unwieldy, that can frighten them" – a somewhat patronizing remark, perhaps, but one that recognized their outstanding talents. De Brosses later commented on the perfection of the symphonic music at the Pietà, stating that the *ospedale* where he went the most often and enjoyed himself the most was the hospital of the Pietà. Jean-Jacques Rousseau was another admirer: he recorded in his *Confessions* (1743) that he could "conceive of nothing as voluptuous, as moving as this music", and commented that "singers from the Venetian opera come so as to develop genuine taste in singing based on these excellent models". He was smitten, too, by the sight of the girls behind "those accursed grilles" that "concealed the angels of loveliness" in the *ospedali* choirs – only to be shocked when permitted to meet a number of them face to face, somewhat unkindly describing them as ugly, blemished, or marked by smallpox. However, after taking time to talk with them, he revised his opinion, stating that he "nearly fell in love with all these ugly girls".

VIRTUOSO AND COMPOSER

As well as being a virtuoso violinist and an inspiring teacher, Vivaldi was also a composer who worked at extraordinary speed, even to the extent of devising a form of musical shorthand. Everything he did in his life was done in a hurry – his handwriting showed signs of haste, and this applied no less to his composing; once a work was completed he was on to the next, unwilling to waste time on anything so mundane as revision. His haste was in part due to the demand by his superiors at the Pietà for a constant supply of fresh music for the *figlie di coro*. Vivaldi wrote between 450 and 500 concertos in his lifetime – leading to an observation, originally made by Italian composer and teacher Dallapiccola, and scathingly taken up by Stravinsky, that Vivaldi was "a tedious man, capable of composing the same concerto six hundred times over".

As we have seen, his concertos catered for a wide variety of instruments. He also composed numerous sonatas, cantatas, and operas, as well as a very considerable number of sinfonias and sacred works, many of which are yet to come to light. It is no wonder that he had to work fast in order to achieve this output and to capture the themes that whirled around in his head. He was far from being the only prolific composer in the Baroque era, however, for in view of the public's continual demand for new music, not to mention the need to earn a living, most composers of the time followed suit. Just a few examples: among much else, J. S. Bach wrote 300 cantatas and Johann Hasse over 100 operas; Domenico Scarlatti produced more than 500 sonatas, and his son Alessandro 100 operas and 600 cantatas. Sammartini is said to have composed a total of 2,800 assorted works, while Telemann is reputed to have been the most prolific of all! The fact that there may inevitably have been a degree of similarity running throughout a composer's works was unimportant, for the public came to accept a particular style and were only too happy, as long as it remained fashionable, to stick to what they were accustomed to.

The two composers whose works most influenced Vivaldi as he started out on his career as a composer were undoubtedly Corelli and Torelli. Arcangelo Corelli (1653–1713) was born into a well-to-do family. He began

John Smith's portrait of Arcangelo
Corelli (1653–1713), one of the
most influential composers of the
Baroque era.

his musical studies in Bologna, and later moved to Rome where he was feted as one of the great violinists of the day and an important composer. Nicknamed "*il divino*", he became chamber musician to ex-Queen Christina of Sweden, later acquiring a new patron in the form of Cardinal Pamphili, said to be the richest man in Rome. When the latter left the city, he acquired the even more prestigious position of director of music to Cardinal Pietro Ottoboni. Written for strings and continuo, much of Corelli's work was divided between the *sonata da camera* (chamber sonata) and the *sonata da chiesa* (church sonata), the former being based on the dance suite, while the latter was more solemn in style, with the organ generally providing the continuo. He published five volumes of chamber music during his life, four of these being sets of trio sonatas and the fifth a set of sonatas for solo violin. He was also to write twelve *concerti grossi* (in which the main part of the orchestra – the *grosso* or *ripieno* – maintains a dialogue with a solo instrument or a small group of instruments – the *concertino*). Eight of these concertos were in solemn style and four based on dance rhythms: they were to become role models for the later Baroque composers, including Vivaldi. Corelli's contemporary, Giuseppi Torelli (1658–1709), spent much of his life in Bologna, where he played the violetta and viol in the cathedral orchestra. An influential composer in the early days of the concerto grosso, to which he had a more progressive attitude than Corelli, he was one of the first to use the ritornello principle (of which more later). He also produced some of the earliest solo concertos for violin, as well as enlivening his works by the inclusion of instruments such as trumpets, horns, and flutes. Whereas Corelli generally composed his concertos in four movements (slow, fast, slow, fast) with two intervals, it was Torelli who was to establish the "Italian

Giuseppi Torelli (1658–1709), an important figure in the development of the concerto grosso and the ritornello principle.

style" three-movement format – allegro, adagio, allegro (fast, slow, fast). This style became the standard for the majority of Vivaldi's concertos, and with the use of this structure the Red Priest was able to create atmospheres and emotions of startling brilliance.

In the earliest days of the Baroque era, sonatas were simply showy instrumental breaks within the opera, usually composed for one or two treble instruments – violins, recorders, or cornets – with a continuo accompaniment, i.e., a bass line supported by keyboard or sundry plucked instruments. However, it was not long before composers began developing these pieces as entities in their own right, and a whole new musical genre was born. Known as the modern style, it heralded the rise of the virtuoso performer, the sonatas and concertos of this period providing a perfect platform for the exhibitionist performer, to the delight of audiences.

By the start of what is now termed the High Baroque in 1700, a sonata would typically consist of three or four extended movements with a pause between each, while most of the bizarre experiments of the previous century had been abandoned. Other common forms from the Baroque period include the suite – an extended sonata or orchestral piece comprising an overture and a selection of dance pieces – minuets, gigues, and the like – and the sinfonia, best described as a sonata for orchestra.

An important figure in the development of the sinfonia is Alessandro Scarlatti (1660–1725). Coming from a poor Neapolitan family, he was to spend much of his later life in Rome, where his patron was the ever-generous Cardinal Ottoboni. Not only did he compose numerous sacred cantatas, serenatas and oratorios, along with over 600 chamber cantatas, but he was also to establish the three-movement sinfonia format as an operatic

Alessandro Scarlatti (1660–1725), member of a family of Italian musicians and a prolific composer. He was a major contributor to the development of the Baroque orchestra.

overture, with a fourth movement in minuet form sometimes added after the slow movement. As the most passionate parts in opera were assigned to the lead singers, however, the sinfonia, in order not to steal their thunder, tended to be a less dramatic work than the concerto. Vivaldi's contemporary Tommaso Albinoni (1671–1751) is also credited with having introduced the minuet into the sinfonia and is regarded as one of the forerunners of the symphonic style. Despite this, he remained a conservative composer and is best remembered, ironically enough, for his Adagio in G Minor; this highly romantic work was apparently put together by Remo Giazotto from fragments of the composer's works – in 1945! The sinfonia was to form the basis of the eighteenth-century symphony, and it is interesting to note that Marc Pincherle suggests that Vivaldi was another composer who had "a determining role in the formulation of the genre".

FIRST PUBLICATIONS

In addition to the instrumental works that he composed for the *figlie di coro*, Vivaldi obtained private commissions whenever he could get them, frequently offering for sale the pieces originally created for the orchestra of the Pietà. Between 1705 and 1709 he was to publish his first two collections, each comprising twelve trio sonatas (this format being the preferred choice of the young composers of the day), scored for violins and basso continuo. These works – his Opus 1 and Opus 2 – were similar in construction to works by Corelli. And although he had not yet developed the distinctive style that was to make his name, Vivaldi was on his way. He dedicated the first collection to the Venetian Count Annibale Gambara. Describing

his Opus 1 as "the first fruits of my feeble efforts", he praised the count's "most excellent and noble family" and, claiming that he possessed "no other adornments than those of my feebleness", begged the count to "deign to accept in respectful tribute these first, most humble products of my labours". His Opus 2 was published in Venice by Antonio Bortoli in 1709. King Frederik IV of Denmark and Norway, who happened to be visiting Venice at the time, attended a performance at the Pietà directed by Vivaldi himself, which he declared to be "very much to his taste". This reception encouraged the composer to write to the king, praising his majestic eminence and humbly asking him to accept the dedication of this new work.

Sire [he wrote], enviable is the fate of a humble heart if it is forced, when it meets a sovereign great by birth, but even greater by virtue, to ensure the multiplicity of his tributes, whatever they are ... Fate could do no more for you than elevate you to such eminence, majesty, and might. But this height does not help the one so far below you; therefore you descended from the throne and your modesty removed the embarrassment of your high position, enabling you to console the one kneeling in front of you who professes to be unworthy of even kissing the lowest step of your throne. Welcome therefore, O great King, not the offer which is in no proportion to your person, but consider the heart that brings it.

The composer signs himself as "Your Majesty's most humble, devoted and obedient servant, Antonio Vivaldi".

Florid letters such as these may seem excessively ingratiating today, but they were an accepted mode of address in the seventeenth and eighteenth centuries. It has to be recognized that in order to survive, composers needed the patronage of the nobles or the church. Every opportunity, therefore, had to be seized upon and maximized. This arrangement usually worked well for all parties, for what cardinal, count, or king could fail to enjoy a little flattery? To be known to have a distinguished patron as a backer increased the repute of the musician or composer, while in the case of the wealthy families, to be seen to support the *ospedali*, to give concerts in their own homes, or to patronize a rising star demonstrated their devotion to charity and the arts. And of course, in common with all Venetians, the music itself gave them great pleasure: what better way to spend their money? Vivaldi's flowery epistles to his dedicatees, therefore, were merely par for the course.

As well as publishing his early works, the Red Priest was fortunate in having the security of his job as *maestro di violino* at the Pietà – at least for a period of six years. However, the position of the male teachers at the Pietà came up every year for review by the chairman and the twelve governors, and had to be agreed by a two-thirds majority vote. In February 1709, Vivaldi failed to secure the requisite number of votes and was forced to leave his post. The reason for his dismissal is unrecorded, but it can be imagined that this fiery, opinionated, impatient, and often tactless member of staff cannot have been the easiest of employees; indeed, he was extremely likely to have put up the backs of several members of the board. So despite the remarkable results he had achieved with the *figlie di coro*, thereby hugely raising the profile of the *ospedale*, Vivaldi suddenly found himself out of a job.

Chapter 5
IN THE WILDERNESS

SACKED!

The shock of his dismissal by the governors of the Pietà hit Vivaldi hard. How, he must have raged, could they have done this to him, he who had lifted the musical standard of the Pietà way above that of the other *ospedali*? The *figlie di coro* were like his own children, whose talents he had nurtured and from whom he was now cut off. How unfair could life be?

The one positive aspect of this setback was that it allowed him a breathing space in which to consider the direction of his future. As the French saying goes: "Il faut reculer pour mieux sauter" ("One must step back in order to leap forward"). Antonio is presumed to have been living at home where his father would have been on hand to advise him on his options – and Giovanni Battista was the ideal person to calm his quick-tempered son's anger at his treatment by the board of the Pietà, and to help him regain his confidence. As a permanent member of the prestigious orchestra of St Mark's – indeed, in 1713 he was listed as one of the best violinists in Venice – Giovanni Battista Vivaldi had contacts in the musical world and years of knowledge of the way in which things worked in the Republic. The fact that the dedication of Vivaldi's Opus 2 had been accepted by King Frederik of Denmark and Norway had given it a certain cachet, and this, along with Vivaldi senior's reputation, no doubt helped Antonio to get a certain amount of work playing in churches and at private concerts and receptions in Venice during the fallow period. Fortunately for musicians, in the course of the close season for opera there was a constant demand for concerts and small-scale dramatic works to be performed in the private *palazzi* and gardens of the nobles. Despite the fact that that *La*

Serenissima had lost her predominance in the Mediterranean, no longer holding "the gorgeous East in fee", the patricians of Venice maintained the standard of living of their forefathers, closing their eyes to the fact that their wealth was no longer flooding in as it had done in the glory days of the Republic. Their entertainments would include lavish meals followed by concerts of instrumental works, along with performances by singers and sometimes even small operas. Additionally, there would be magnificent spectacles to celebrate almost any important event in the history of the Republic of Venice, from the election of a new doge or other important official down to something as bizarre as a commemoration of the centenary of the devastating plague of 1630, which swept over Venice killing a third of its population: literally, any excuse for a party. These festivities were encouraged by officials as being a means of keeping the populace happy; the more they were involved in pleasurable activities, the less likely they would be to start rebelling against the uniquely repressive powers of the government. The foreign embassies – of whom there were many, Venice being a desirable posting and something of an *entrepôt* for intelligence-gathering – also vied with one another in their grand lifestyles and in the magnificence of their ceremonies in celebration of important events taking place in their own countries.

The fact of Vivaldi's dismissal from the Pietà soon became known throughout the city, however, and this fact, along with his humble background, would have done little to help him effectively to penetrate far into the closed shop of the nobles. Indeed, since before medieval times, musicians had been regarded as providing a mere service, and it was many years before they would receive adequate respect for their skills, regardless

George Frederick
Handel, by Philippe
Mercier, c. 1730.
Handel's early works
were performed in
Italy, although much of
his later life was spent
in England.

of their social standing – an attitude of mind that would doubtless have infuriated the Red Priest.

At around the time that Vivaldi lost his job at the Pietà, the young composer George Frederick Handel arrived in Venice (in a winter so cold that the canals froze over) to present his opera *Agrippina* during the Carnival season. Its enthusiastic reception – twenty-seven performances in Venice alone, and then on to further towns and cities in Italy and other countries of Europe – came as a further blow to the demoralized priest; the last thing he needed at his lowest point was to witness the triumph of a young rival in the world of music. It would be surprising if the two composers had not met on this occasion, for they were much of an age and following the same profession. Certainly Vivaldi would have attended a performance of *Agrippina*, and there is no doubt that the opera's success led him and his father to give serious attention to this alternative, and very popular, musical genre. Indeed, Giovanni Battista, with an eye to its money-making potential, had for some time seen opera as the way forward, for it was clear that the public could not get enough of this particular form of entertainment. Last year's opera was dead in the water; what the audiences wanted, year in year out, was something new. Many operas were not even written down, such was their ephemeral nature.

Antonio, by contrast, was more inclined to sink his energies into the composing of concertos, where he felt he had the greatest talent. In his depressed state, however, he was for a time lacking in inspiration and finding it hard to get down to work of any kind. It was not until he had begun to recover from the injustice of having the ground cut from under his feet by the board of the Pietà that he recognized that a new challenge

This late eighteenth-century engraving depicts the palace of Prince Ruspoli in Rome. Francesco Gasparini became *maestro di cappella* to the Prince following his departure from the Pietà.

... it was during his spell in the wilderness that Vivaldi began to compose concertos again – and this time with outstanding success.

was just what he needed. While teaching the *figlie di coro*, he had always been more in tune with instrumental rather than with choral music, although his experience of working at the Pietà with a combination of voices and instruments would have stood him in good stead when he came seriously to consider the world of opera. But notwithstanding the fact that opera had begun to beckon, it was during his spell in the wilderness that Vivaldi began to compose concertos again – and this time with outstanding success.

REINSTATED

As so often happens, a run of disasters can be followed by a spell of good fortune. Certainly this was so in the Red Priest's case. Having experienced the anger and depression of his dismissal and his failure to gain the recognition of the musical world of Venice that he felt he deserved, the ambitious young man started with a sudden burst of creativity to put together some new instrumental works. He had additionally begun toying with ideas for an opera when, in September 1711, he was recalled to the Pietà by the unanimous vote of the board of governors. During his absence some temporary and ineffective replacements had been appointed; however, it had soon become obvious to the governors that the reputation of the *ospedale* was slipping, and it had to be admitted, even if grudgingly, that no matter how tiresome the Red Priest might on occasion be, his talents as a teacher were undeniable. The minutes of the board stated: "Realizing the necessity of securing ever better instrumental tuition for the girls studying music in order to increase the reputation of the pious establishment, the post of violin master being vacant, we move that Dom Antonio Vivaldi be appointed violin master at an annual salary of 60 ducats..."

It is likely that Gasparini had something to do with Vivaldi's reinstatement, seeing the younger man as his escape route. For, while undertaking his demanding role over many years as *maestro di coro* at the Pietà, Gasparini had become increasingly involved in composing for opera. In 1713 he determined to leave Venice, in part for health reasons but also in order to spread his wings by working in other cities. He was given a brief leave of absence from the Pietà, from which he never effectively returned, eventually taking the post of *maestro di cappella* to Prince Ruspoli in Rome.

In his absence, more and more composing work fell to the lot of the Red Priest. Finally, without actually awarding him the title of *maestro di coro* – a step too far, perhaps? – the board of governors came to expect Vivaldi to provide pretty well everything that had been required of Gasparini, namely a new mass and vespers for the feasts of Easter and the Visitation of the Blessed Virgin respectively, an oratorio and over thirty motets a year, plus compositions for any other occasions that might crop up. In recognition of this extra work, "this pious congregation", as the board of governors liked to describe themselves, saw fit "in its generosity to award him a token of gratitude and recompense him in part for these services outside his normal duties" with "a single payment of 50 ducats". Furthermore, they expressed the hope that this reward might stimulate him "to make further contributions and to perfect still more the performing abilities of the girls". Perhaps the girls, too, had something to do with the reinstatement of their inspiring teacher. Whatever the case, the period in the wilderness was over. *Il Prete Rosso* was back in town!

Chapter 6
THE ARTS OF THE BAROQUE

DEVELOPMENTS IN MUSIC

With Vivaldi back at the Pietà, it is perhaps a good moment to pause and take a look at his musical heritage in a little more detail, in order to understand the changes that had taken place prior to his arrival on the scene, and the direction in which he was to go as a result. The age into which the Red Priest was born is nowadays referred to in music and art as the Baroque – a somewhat derogatory term when one looks at the meaning of the word: irregular, bizarre, or even rough and coarse, and said to derive from the Portuguese *barocco*, meaning a "misshapen pearl". The term was first coined by early twentieth-century historians to describe a musical style that was arguably at that time little understood and viewed merely as a primitive forerunner to the works of the great classical masters. Yet this description still stands today as the official classification of all music from 1600 to 1740.

Although touched upon by the Renaissance composers, the concept of harmony specifically used to depict emotion and drama is one of the principal features of the Baroque era that followed. From the beginning of the Early Baroque composers began to experiment, often wildly, with harmony, taking pleasure in the use of dissonance (jarring combinations of notes) for dramatic effect. At the same time came the beginnings of a more emotive approach to performance in general, with musicians expected to study the science of rhetoric and to apply the techniques to their playing and singing, employing a vivid use of light and shade and often a highly flexible approach to rhythm, in order to heighten the emotional impact of the delivery. In this way, the Baroque period could be described as the era of *conscious emotion* in music.

Although some scholars today consider that Baroque music is all about artifice – that is, emotions projected by the performer in an objective, almost detached manner – yet there is plentiful evidence to the contrary, and it appears undeniable that the star performers of the day performed with heartfelt intensity. Indeed, in 1702 a performance by the renowned violinist Corelli, who, as we have seen, was instrumental along with his contemporary Torelli in developing the musical genre that was to provide Vivaldi a few years later with his most successful format, was described by Ragunet thus: "I never met with any man that suffered his passions to hurry him away so much while he was playing on the violin as the famous Arcangelo Corelli, whose eyes will sometimes turn as red as fire; his countenance will be distorted, his eyeballs roll as in agony, and he gives so much to what he is doing that he doth not look like the same man." Towards the end of the High Baroque period, C. P. E. Bach was similarly to write that "a musician cannot move others unless he too is moved; he must of necessity feel all of the affects he hopes to arouse in his audience". For Vivaldi, a man whose passionate nature drew him inexorably towards dramatic modes of expression, the High Baroque provided the perfect stage. Not only was he a composer whose works would outlive those of many of his contemporaries, but he was also nothing less than a virtuoso performer whose dazzling skills in his particular field would make him sought after throughout Europe.

A further distinguishing feature of Baroque music was the degree of ornamentation that it incorporated. This demand put heavy pressure on the performer, requiring study of the many different forms of embellishment that had to be added at key places, such as at "cadence points" (i.e. the last

The church of SS Giovanni and Paolo,
commonly known as San Zanipolo.
Outside stands the famous equestrian
statue of the mercenary, Bartolomeo
Colleoni.

few bars of each section of the piece). German flautist and writer
Johann Joachim Quantz was to comment that Italian composers
wrote certain passages very simply, in order that the player could
vary them as he pleased. These embellishments developed quite
differently in Germany, France, and Italy. Thus the skill required
by the performer in learning how to play the different styles and
in incorporating them effortlessly into the music so that they
sounded like improvisation was demanding to say the least. It
was, however, a technique that the Red Priest made his own.

ART IN VENICE

It would be interesting to know the extent to which Vivaldi was
inspired in his musical career by the beauty of his surroundings
in *La Serenissima*. While nothing is known of his interests outside
the world of music, yet, like the Venetian painters, his patrimony
was the light and shade reflected in the rippling waters, the deep
shadows cast on to the canals by the *palazzi*, the shapes of the
boats on the lagoon, and the changing colours of the skies that
stretched away to the outer islands. Splendour in the form of
buildings, sculpture, and art of all kinds surrounded him every
day at every turn.

    Heading westwards from the family home that faced the
square on which stood the church of San Giovanni in Bragora –
the church in which he had been baptized for the second time –
Vivaldi would soon have reached the Pietà, a journey he must have

made many hundreds of times in his life. How familiar he would have been with the decorative elements of the original chapel! Walking further along the Riva degli Schiavoni – though, bearing in mind his chest complaint, he would perhaps have taken a carriage or gondola in later years – he would have passed the superb façades of the *palazzi* that faced on to St Mark's canal, before reaching the stunningly gothic Doge's Palace. Just around the corner he would have arrived at the Piazza San Marco, where St Mark's Basilica stood in all its breathtaking ornamentation and golden glory.

Left: The Resurrection by Alvise Vivarini (c.1445–1503). It can be seen in the church of San Giovanni in Bragora, Venice.
Below: The church of San Giovanni in Bragora, near Antonio Vivaldi's family home, and where he was baptized.

Having performed there from an early age, he could hardly fail to have been influenced by the extraordinary richness of its decor both inside and out.

During his training as a priest, the young Antonio would also have become acquainted with the churches near his home. The fifteenth-century San Giovanni in Bragora was familiar to him, its name being variously said to derive from the words for "mud" and "stagnant canal", from the verb "to fish", from the Greek *agora* (marketplace), and from a region in the East said to be home to the relics of St John the Baptist, this latter perhaps the most tasteful interpretation. Supposedly founded in the eighth century, the outer appearance of the church dated from 1475, while the interior boasted, among other works of art, Alvise Vivarini's painting of the Resurrection. Not far off was the somewhat grander church of SS Giovanni e Paolo (known in Venetian dialect as San Zanipolo), in which Vivaldi would

The west facade of the Doge's
Palace in Venice, lining the Piazza
San Marco.

have seen superb works by other Venetian painters including Giovanni
Bellini, Lorenzo Lotti, and Paolo Veronese. Inspired by the unique light of
Venice, the painters of the Venetian school had, over two centuries or more,
developed a distinctive style that combined a love of deep, rich colour with
soft, sometimes almost impressionistic brushstrokes. Contemporary with
Vivaldi were painters Tiepolo, Canaletto, and Guardi – as brilliant in their
own fields as Vivaldi was in his. The latter two were to produce memorable
vedute – detailed scenes of festivals on the canals and ceremonies in the
Piazza San Marco – that would have been more than familiar to the Red
Priest. There were numerous other churches on the Rialto, all displaying
their treasures. In addition to his work at the Pietà, Vivaldi, as we have
seen, also performed in private concerts for the nobles in some of the grand
palazzi that boasted their own superb collections of art. Who can say what
effect this profusion of artistic splendour may have had on the young
musician and composer?

SUMMER

Chapter 7

SECULAR MUSIC

L'ESTRO ARMONICO

In the year 1711, Vivaldi's star was again in the ascendant. Not only was he restored to the position of *maestro di violino* to the *figlie di coro* at the Pietà, but the work that was to make the Venetians first sit up and take notice – his Opus 3, entitled *L'Estro Armonico* (The Harmonic Fancy) – was launched on to the musical stage in 1712. This collection of solo concertos was marked by Vivaldi's extraordinary vitality and forceful rhythms, and overflowed with the emotions that poured forth in torrents from the fast movements and sang with spellbinding beauty in the slow ones. It was this work that set him on the road to becoming one of the major musical influences of his time, an influence that would have an effect on composers for many years ahead.

The concerto grosso of the Middle Baroque period, as demonstrated by the works of Corelli and his contemporaries, tended to be a relatively calm and ordered affair, generally featuring a group of strings accompanied by a full string orchestra, with no single voice predominating (for, despite throwing himself heart and soul into his performance, as described earlier, Corelli nevertheless maintained a degree of impersonality in his compositions). By contrast, the solo concerto gave precedence to a single solo instrument (or sometimes two contrasted instruments, and even on occasion as many as four solo violins, for example) with orchestral backing. With this difference in focus, pictures and emotions could be expressed more vividly through the music. As far as instruments were concerned, Vivaldi's own preference was always for the violin; however, he never failed to cater for the girls of the Pietà, and his solo concertos would include virtuoso elements for the variety of instruments played by his phenomenally talented students.

Vivaldi is thought to have studied with Corelli; whether or not this was
so, certainly the latter's influence was apparent in many of the younger
man's early trio sonatas and concertos. But it was with *L'Estro Armonico* that
the Red Priest found the sound that he was looking for – a sound that was
to become his distinctive voice. From now on he was generally to adopt the
three-movement style in his concertos (although with occasional exceptions
– sometimes including two slow movements or two final allegros). With the
concertos included in Opus 3 he broke from earlier tradition to demonstrate
his free spirit and individualism; it was here that he was to make use of the
ritornello principle (of which more below) to express the conversation –
the conflict, even – between the solo and orchestral parts. The work was
dedicated to Grand Prince Ferdinand III of Tuscany. After apologies for
the poor quality of the printing of his earlier works and assurances that
under "the famous hand of Monsieur Estienne Roger" all would in future
be well, the offering was accompanied by the usual ingratiating and self-
deprecating preface. "Your Royal Highness," he began, "this opus may gain
but little approval from your knowledgeable, formidable and truly sovereign
judgment, but it is offered with all the devotion of a humble heart to the
boundless merit of Your Royal Highness, although it bears no proportion
to your venerable greatness." And so on. Ferdinand was a keen amateur
musician himself and already a patron of the Scarlattis, Albinoni, and
Handel – obviously a man whose goodwill was worth cultivating.

It was indeed to Vivaldi's great good fortune that *L'Estro Armonico* was
published by Estienne Roger, a French resident of Amsterdam, who had
founded his own music-publishing business and was on the lookout for
new clients. Although Italy had pioneered the concept of lined manuscript

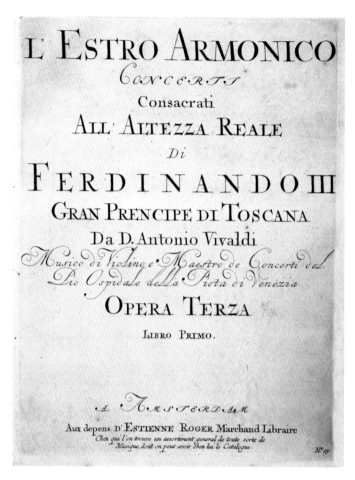

L' ESTRO ARMONICO

Concerti

Consacrati

ALL' ALTEZZA REALE

Di

FERDINANDO III

GRAN PRENCIPE DI TOSCANA

Da D. Antonio Vivaldi

Musico di Violino e Maestro de Concerti del Pio Ospidale della Pietà di Venezia

OPERA TERZA

LIBRO PRIMO.

A AMSTERDAM

Aux depens D'ESTIENNE ROGER Marchand Libraire
Chez qui l'on trouve un assortiment general de toute sorte de Musique, dont on peut avoir chez lui le Catalogue.

N.° 50

paper, scores were still printed there with movable type, an awkward and lengthy practice that produced less than satisfactory results. Now, in both London and Amsterdam, the process of engraving on to copper plates had been established, resulting in a high-quality end product. Not only did Estienne Roger offer a printing service, but he also published and distributed the scores throughout Europe, with royalties going to the composers. In addition, he was not above pirating works already published in Italy. Fortunately, Vivaldi soon became one of his valued clients, along with Corelli, Albinoni, Alessandro Scarlatti, and other luminaries of the Baroque. The company's catalogues were widely distributed, causing interest in Italian music to spread rapidly to an audience way beyond that country's borders. On Roger's death, the firm was taken over by his son-in-law, Michel-Charles Le Cène, and its clientele expanded to include Handel and Telemann among others. At the same time, in London, John Walsh was offering a similar publishing service, his business being responsible for the printing of many of Handel's later works. Italy and Germany would not become active in the music-publishing scene until the early nineteenth century.

LA STRAVAGANZA

Vivaldi's Opus 4 – *La Stravaganza* (The Extravagance) – was published in 1713/1714. This collection of twelve exhilarating violin concertos further enhanced the Red Priest's reputation. While maintaining the necessary degree of discipline and symmetry, his bold and imaginative compositions were stimulated by the theatrical drama of opera, and his own flamboyant virtuosity on the violin led him to include equally virtuosic elements for the solo parts. Johann Joachim Quantz first came across Vivaldi's concertos at this time, describing them as an entirely novel type of musical composition and stating that he made sure to collect a good number of them. One learns from the comments of some of his visitors that Vivaldi was known by those who wished to purchase his works to be a man who drove a hard bargain, a fact that was to become ever more pronounced as his reputation and popularity increased. He appears to have been permanently obsessed by the need to acquire money, a need no doubt stemming from a lack of financial security in his childhood and the requirement in adulthood to contribute to the support of his family – and later perhaps, also to that of the Giro sisters. In true Venetian style, therefore, he was not above using a certain

It was fortunate... that his clients were so thrilled by the novelty of his music that they could overlook his deceit, his volatile moods, and his financial rapacity.

amount of deceit in its acquisition. This fact was particularly evident as he dashed his concertos off at speed – not infrequently rehashing them from earlier works – and sold them as new for outrageous sums to rich friends and admirers. It was fortunate, perhaps, that his clients were so thrilled by the novelty of his music that they could overlook his deceit, his volatile moods, and his financial rapacity.

It was around the time of the publication of *La Stravaganza* that a number of German and Czech violinists and virtuosos came to study in Venice, where they were inevitably influenced by the musical style of Antonio Vivaldi. One such visitor was Johann Friedrich Armand von Uffenbach, a distinguished architect and amateur musician from Frankfurt-am-Main. Having been encouraged by the response to his presentation of *L'Estro Armonico* at a Strasburg music society in 1715, Uffenbach decided to pay a visit to the home of its progenitor – Venice. Here he heard Vivaldi play an improvised cadenza in the Sant'Angelo theatre (for by this date the Red Priest had begun to become involved in opera), after which he commented that it really frightened him, "for such playing has never been nor can be: he brought his fingers up to only a straw's distance from the bridge, leaving no room for the bow – and that on all four strings with imitations and incredible speed. With this he astounded everyone, but I cannot say that it pleased me, for it was not so pleasant to listen to as it was skilfully executed." Obviously a man who preferred the conventional to the virtuosic, Uffenbach was nevertheless sufficiently entranced that he called on the composer, saying that he would like to order some concerti grossi from him. Never one to let the grass grow under his feet, within three days Vivaldi brought along ten works that he claimed to have composed especially for his visitor. Doubtless these concertos were retrieved from his library – although it is worth remembering that the speedy priest boasted that he could compose a concerto quicker than a copyist could copy it; indeed, he would also later announce that he had written a complete opera in just five days. On this occasion, Uffenbach, though sceptical, was clearly happy, as he bought some of the works (in addition to having had a few bottles of wine fetched for the composer, "knowing that he was a cleric" – clerics presumably being in permanent need of wine). Vivaldi, never one to miss an opportunity, additionally arranged to give occasional lessons to his admirer.

Among the German violinists who journeyed to Venice to make the acquaintance of the Red Priest was Johann Georg Pisendel. Said to be one of his most satisfied pupils and the one most affected by his teaching, Pisendel was a violin virtuoso and member of a group of chamber musicians who spent some time in Venice in 1716 and 1717. He recounts playing a Vivaldi violin concerto – fast enough at the best of times – between acts in an opera, during which the orchestra speeded up the accompaniment in order to thoroughly discomfort the visitor; Pisendel, however, stamped his feet loudly in the

St Mark's Square at dusk.

correct tempo, thus putting the orchestra itself to shame. Obviously the two men got on well, for on another occasion, Pisendel was walking in the Piazza San Marco with Vivaldi when the composer suddenly whisked him away, explaining that they were being followed by four policemen. Once in the safety of his home, he asked Pisendel if he had committed any crime in Venice. The German being unable to think of anything, Vivaldi suggested his companion remain in the house while he carried out some investigations. It turned out that the State Inquisitors had mistaken Pisendel for someone for whom they were searching – clear evidence that in pleasure-loving Venice, strict surveillance was very much the order of the day.

On his return to Germany, Pisendel became leader of the Dresden Court orchestra, where he maintained Vivaldi's instrumental works in place of honour in its repertoire, making Dresden, as Michael Talbot records in his biography of the composer "the centre of the Vivaldian cult in Germany." The two violinists remained friends to the extent that over the years Vivaldi dedicated eleven works to his former pupil, the manuscripts marked *Fatto per il Sigr. Pisendel*. At the same time as the rise in popularity of his orchestral music, Vivaldi's church music also made its mark in Dresden.

It can be seen from the growing appreciation of his works in Venice, and from the increasing number of visitors from abroad who came to make his acquaintance and to hear his music, that Vivaldi's distinctive style (of which more below) was becoming well established and widely admired. In 1717 his Opus 6, comprising six scores that were among some pieces that he had earlier sent to Amsterdam, was collated and published under the imprint of Roger's daughter Jeanne, to meet the growing demand for new works. Included in this collection is the *Cuckoo Concerto*, which became particularly popular in England in the early eighteenth century: Charles Burney relates how this concerto had been "the wonder and delight of all frequenters of country concerts". As well as the concertos named after the cuckoo (Opus 6) and the goldfinch (Opus 10), birds of varying descriptions also make their appearance in *The Four Seasons*. One can imagine how these light-hearted pieces must have delighted the girls at the Pietà!

A WINNING FORMULA

What was it that caused Vivaldi's orchestral works, and in particular his concertos, to become so popular? And what were the techniques he used to achieve his winning formula?

It can be said that much of the Red Priest's success with his orchestral works stemmed from his clever use of the ritornello principle. The ritornello was found in many forms such as fugues and operatic arias during the Baroque era. And just as Torelli's work inspired Vivaldi to adopt the three-movement concerto, it was also almost certainly his example that brought the ritornello to Vivaldi's attention. By embracing the concept in his concertos, the Red Priest was to achieve some of his most outstanding successes and to write music of enormous creativity and variety.

The ritornello, which can be translated as a "little something that returns", is basically a passage of music that recurs time and again, either in full or in part, this repetition acting as a unifying factor within the concerto. The recurrent section, performed by the full orchestra (the *tutti*), alternates and contrasts with the *episodes* or sections performed by the solo instrument or group of solo instruments also known as the *concertino*.

Thus, a movement would start with the tutti playing the ritornello in full, followed by a solo (either with continuo or upper string accompaniment), then a section of the ritornello, another solo episode, another section of the ritornello, and so on, this dialogue continuing perhaps three or four times throughout the piece, the movement always ending with a return to the ritornello.

Vivaldi uses this process to move elegantly though a cycle of keys: the tutti starts by playing the first section in, let us say, the key of C. The soloist section starts in the key of C but ends in a new key, say G. The tutti then both starts and finishes in G. The second solo section starts in G but ends in, for example, A minor. The tutti begins and ends in A minor. The final solo section starts in A minor but finishes, in a pleasingly circular fashion, in the key of C, enabling the tutti to end the final movement with a flourish in the original key. It has been suggested that the tutti existed merely to allow the soloist a rest; Vivaldi, however, was to allot to the tutti a vigorous part in the musical conversation. This constantly recurring theme gives the listener an instant handle on the structure of the piece.

The majority of the opening movements in Vivaldi's concertos are in ritornello format, usually played fast for dramatic effect. The second – slow – movement provides a total contrast, without the ritornello and with the soloist often playing in lyrical style. In the third movement, the ritornello principle returns, but with a different theme. It is perhaps unsurprising to discover that in the Red Priest's concertos the solo player is generally a showy virtuoso who is given a more prominent role throughout than in earlier works of this nature.

Although this was the basic structure of Vivaldi's concertos, it must be said that he not infrequently broke his own rules, and it was this unexpected approach that made him such an interesting composer. One example is the famous flute concerto *La Notte* (the Night) from Opus 8: this weird and disturbing work is in six sections and sounds more like a Hammer House of Horror movie score than a Baroque concerto. In another case (RV565 – one of the concertos from *L'Estro Armonico*), the opening consists of a series of short virtuoso vignettes, followed by a rather Germanic-sounding fugue – the ritornello only appearing in the last movement.

THE FOUR SEASONS

In 1725, Le Cène published Vivaldi's Opus 8 – *Il Cimento dell'Armonia e dell'Invenzione* (The Contest between Harmony and Invention) – which was to become the composer's most popular work. In this further collection of twelve solo concertos, seven were descriptive, although it is the first four of these – *Le Quattro Stagioni* (The Four Seasons) – that are the most universally recognized, not only providing many people with an introduction to the music of Vivaldi, but also serving as his lasting memorial.

The Four Seasons must be one of the most descriptive pieces of music ever composed, even if nowadays it is all too often hackneyed by its use as ambient muzak and "please don't hang up" background music on the telephone. But these uses are best forgotten, and the work remembered for its colour and inventiveness, its vivid descriptions, its richly painted canvas, its contrasts, and the emotions that it engenders. Feel the cold, the breeze, the heat, the lethargy; hear the thunder, the cracking ice, and the buzzing flies; enjoy the dance, the wine, the thrill of the chase, the sleep...! *Le Quattro*

Stagioni was composed around four sonnets possibly written by Vivaldi himself and scored for solo violin with the orchestra consisting of violins, violas, violoncellos, and double basses, plus continuo. The four concertos, each in the fast-slow-fast format, evoke the moods, sounds, and events of the seasons. As with many of Vivaldi's concertos, much use is made of the ritornello principle, in which, as we have seen, the solo and tutti – in this case the full orchestra – sections alternate, the *tutti* and the solo instrument being based on the same material.

With the sonnets in mind as we listen, the music causes vivid pictures to arise before our eyes, and we not only visualize the peasants' pastoral idyll as it progresses through the year, but also become aware of the misery caused by the intense heat of a Venetian summer, the raging storms, and the bitter cold of winter. In "Spring" the string orchestra contrasts with the solo violin: first we hear the birds singing, followed by a storm; then the viola plays the part of a vigorously barking dog, and finally the peasants dance to the sound of bagpipes. "Summer" starts dreamily with more birdsong; gnats and flies start to buzz, and a north wind blows, heralding another storm; as it approaches we hear the plaint of the shepherd, who fears for his flock. In "Autumn" the continuo includes the bassoon, creating a rustic atmosphere. There is dancing until the revellers fall into a drunken sleep; at dawn they awake to the sound of the hunters, who chase and finally kill an exhausted deer. The violins of "Winter" imitate freezing winds, stamping feet and chattering teeth, followed by escape to a warm fireside; the movement ends with a scene of jollity as the peasants slide on the ice then return indoors to escape the north wind.

La Primavera (Spring)

Allegro

Spring has come, greeted by the birds
Who celebrate her return with their cheerful songs,
While gentle breezes caress the murmuring streams.
Then thunder and lightning, heralds of spring,
Cover the heavens with a dark cloak.
Once they have died away
The birds return to their enchanting song.

Largo

On the flowery meadows, while branches rustle overhead,
A goatherd sleeps,
His faithful dog at his side.

Allegro

To the festive sound of rustic bagpipes
Nymphs and shepherds dance
Beneath the brilliant canopy of spring.

Left: Red tile rooftops cover the city of Venice
beneath the dome of St Mark's Basicilia.
Right: The Grand Canal.

L'Estate (Summer)

Allegro non molto

Under the harsh heat of the sun
Men and flocks swelter and the pines burn.
We hear the voice of the cuckoo,
Then the sweet songs of the turtle-dove and goldfinch.
A soft breeze stirs the air then is swept aside
By the threatening north wind.
The shepherd cries out, fearing a violent storm and his fate.

Adagio e piano – Presto e forte

His tired limbs are stirred from sleep
By the flash of lightning and the roar of thunder –
And by a swarm of angry buzzing gnats and flies.

Presto

Alas, his fears are justified:
The heavens thunder and hailstones flatten the ears of corn.

Misty morning with gondolas by
St Mark's Square, Venice.
Opposite: The church of Santa Maria
della Salute after snowfall.

L'Automno (Autumn)

Allegro

The peasants celebrate with song and dance
The pleasure of harvest safely gathered in.
Filled with the liquor of Bacchus
Many slide into a deep slumber.

Adagio molto

As cooling breezes stir the air,
The singing and dancing die away.
The season invites all to enjoy a sweet sleep.

Allegro

The hunters are out at dawn, ready for the chase,
With horns, guns and dogs.
The deer flees as they follow its trail.
Terrified and wounded, it struggles on
Until eventually, exhausted, it dies.

L'Inverno (Winter)

Allegro non molto

Shivering with cold in the frozen snow
And the harsh breath of an icy wind.
Running to and fro, stamping our feet,
Teeth chattering in the bitter chill.

Largo

Resting contentedly by the hearth,
While outside the rain pours down.

Allegro

We walk slowly on the icy path, for fear of falling.
We turn abruptly, slip, and crash to the ground.
Rising, we hurry across the ice before it cracks and breaks up.
We feel the chill north wind through our locked and bolted doors.
This is winter – but despite all, what joy it brings!

The title *Il Cimento dell'Armonia e dell'Invenzione* could also be translated as "The Contest between Rationality and Fantasy". For while Vivaldi's imagination triumphed over the strict rules of composition, the more fantastic elements of his creativity were still subject to a degree of rationality, as shown in his use of the ritornello principle. It was his imagination, though, that created the pictures painted by The Four Seasons – pictures that would many years later provide the inspiration behind Beethoven's Pastoral Symphony.

In the same collection we can capture images of *Il Piacere* (Pleasure) and *La Caccia* (The Hunt), and can feel ourselves tossed fearfully on the waves in *La Tempesta di Mare* (The Storm at Sea). In 1728 he published Opus 9, a set of six violin concertos entitled *La Cetra* (The Lyre), followed by Opus 10, a further six concertos for flute and strings – two collections in which we are condemned to alternate between the uneasy sleep and fearful nightmares of *La Notte*, or, by contrast, to surrender ourselves to the enchanting song of *Il Gardelino* (The Goldfinch). He was to publish a further six violin concertos in Opus 11, followed by a short Opus 12.

Vivaldi continued to produce a considerable amount of instrumental music throughout his life, although a fair degree of recycling of good tunes was involved. As we have seen, wind instruments featured strongly in the earlier works, these being popular among the girls of the Pietà. Unsurprisingly, many of his compositions were for strings, in particular the violin, while his later cello concertos were said by musicologist Michael Talbot to "tower above those of his contemporaries". By this time, Vivaldi's work was having a considerable influence on the German musical scene, where he was to inspire the young Johann Sebastian Bach and the flautist Johann Joachim Quantz, among others.

Chapter 8
SACRED MUSIC

RELIGIOUS CELEBRATIONS

The eighteenth-century professor of music at Oxford, William Hayes, once complained that Antonio Vivaldi was a man with "too much mercury in his system". Certainly the composer's lifestyle was far from that of a conventional priest, yet despite his immersion in instrumental music and his later move into the more commercial world of opera, he never totally forwent his priestly role as he saw it, maintaining his connection with the Pietà – for whom he wrote most of his sacred music – for almost all of his life. What is more, Marc Pincherle describes him as "exaggeratedly devout", putting down his rosary only to take up his pen to write. This comment contrasts with the views of his detractors, as we shall see later, and we shall never know for sure the extent of the Red Priest's commitment to his profession. Much of his behaviour was certainly on the worldly side, although that was a typically Venetian trait. Yet when it came to composing his religious works, he revealed a depth of feeling and sincerity that cannot be denied. Certainly he attempted to sell his works for the highest possible sums, as extant correspondence demonstrates. Yet at the same time, the spirituality that is so evident in his sacred works bears out biographer H. C. Robbins Landon's words that "Vivaldi was above everything else a priest in the Holy Roman Catholic church".

The Red Priest's lengthy induction into the priesthood and his years spent training the girls to perform in the chapel of the Pietà must have had a powerful effect on the young man; and although it may not have been his choice to enter the church, as things turned out he was able to combine his spiritual training with his passion for music. Thus it can be said that as a priest he expressed his devotions through his musical compositions rather than more conventionally in the performance of the mass. Certainly his sacred music displays a unique expression of faith while at the same time containing much of the rhythm, colour, and emotion of his secular works – including the use of the ritornello, in which he contrasts the solo singers with the chorus. It is significant that whereas his operas have for the most part sunk without trace, his sacred music has become highly regarded some 270 years after his death.

Throughout the time that he was composing his concertos at the Pietà, Vivaldi was also writing music for sacred occasions – some forty to fifty major pieces in all – most of it initially for performance by the *figlie di coro*. As we have seen, in the year or so after Gasparini's departure from the Pietà in 1711, he had already composed a mass, vespers, an oratorio, and thirty motets for the *ospedale*. There would, of course, be plenty of opportunities for these sacred works to be performed elsewhere, for, unlike in the world of opera, there was no closed season in the Christian calendar: solemn festivals in celebration of important religious occasions continued year round.

The inhabitants of the Republic were said to be "Venetians first, then Christians", and in religious matters as well as in government, *La Serenissima* had always been determined to maintain her independence. This attitude, stemming from Venice's early links with Byzantium rather than Rome, was to cause conflict with the papacy. Indeed, the refusal of the Republic's authorities to search out and execute heretics led to the Venetians being threatened with or actually suffering the interdict (the removal of the right to the sacraments) on several occasions – a threat that was blithely ignored.

But however fractious the relationship with Rome may have been, the Venetians continued to mark the Christian festivals throughout the

year with their usual fervour. Each of the Republic's seventy-odd parish churches, sprinkled across the Rialto and the islands of the Lagoon, put on the most lavish displays for its patronal feast day, as well as for other major occasions in the Christian calendar. These events were pure theatre, with processions of richly clad Venetians, fleets of gondolas, bearers of torches and relics, and decorations inside the churches and out: the more prestigious the church, the more splendid the celebrations. This display of pomp and glory was designed to attract the crowds and to remind them of the magnificence of their Christian heritage – although it has to be said that many of the people who flocked to these spectacular events regarded them merely as further occasions for pleasure; for often in the evenings food would be laid out, wine would flow, and the Venetians, masked as for Carnival, would give themselves over yet again to a night of sensual delight.

One of Venice's most important patronal feasts was that of the *Solemnita* of San Lorenzo, for which Vivaldi's concerto in C major (RV 556) was specifically written. The convent of San Lorenzo housed many nuns whose aristocratic families wanted to avoid paying a large dowry on their marriage; a way out of this problem was to settle one or more daughters in a convent for which a much smaller dowry was required. Since they housed many patrician inmates, these upper-class Venetian convents were places of considerable comfort, in some cases the nuns' parlour resembling the drawing room of a *palazzo*. Here the cloistered girls, while seated behind a grille, could converse with members of their families, offering them cakes and biscuits that they had baked themselves, while keeping up with the gossip. A picture painted by Francesco Guardi depicts one such nuns' parlour, that of the convent of San Zaccaria. During the Carnival season the nuns were permitted to watch, from within their enclosure, a ball or opera taking place in the parlour. In addition to the music that formed part of the religious services, they would on celebratory occasions also enjoy concerts of instrumental works, in particular the solo concerto.

Music, of course – sacred music of the highest quality – played an essential part in all the religious celebrations of the time. According to Aristotle, "some people fall into a religious frenzy" as a result of listening to sacred melodies, and are "restored as though they had found healing and purgation". Sacred music throughout the centuries has been regarded as providing both food for the artistic senses and food for the soul; meeting this need for music was to provide work for Vivaldi and for many composers and musicians in the Baroque age, as it had in the Renaissance era that preceded it. Although Vivaldi had not set out at the beginning of his career to write church music, it was as a result of his employment at

Francesco Guardi's painting shows the nuns at San Zaccaria conversing with their aristrocratic visitors from behind the grille.

the Pietà that he discovered a talent for the genre. Thus his sacred works, in addition to forming an important part of the repertoire of the *figlie di coro* at the *ospedale*, were also performed in the religious celebrations at St Mark's and at other churches in Venice and abroad.

ST MARK'S BASILICA

The Basilica of St Mark, by virtue of its location and its extraordinary presence, provided the focal point for religious ceremonies in Venice, despite the fact that its dependence upon the doge rather than the patriarch prevented it from holding the title of cathedral until 1807. In 1457 Venice had become a patriarchy, the bishop of Venice receiving the prestigious title of patriarch and becoming responsible for the Roman rite. His cathedral – San Pietro di Castello – was sited on an island to the east of the Rialto. The chaplain to the doge, known as the *primicerio*, was chosen from the ranks of the nobles and based in St Mark's Basilica, where he was responsible for the celebration of the Venetian or "Marcian" rite.

Gentile Bellini's (1429–1507)
painting of the *Procession of the
True Cross in St Mark's Square*.

The first church dedicated to St Mark the Evangelist had been built in 832 near the doge's palace, as a mausoleum to hold the body of the saint when it arrived in Venice following its theft from Alexandria by the Venetians. The prestigious St Mark, with his symbol of a winged lion, rapidly replaced his predecessor, the obscure Greek warrior St Theodore accompanied by his dragon-cum-crocodile, to become the patron saint of the city. Both the doge's palace and the church were burnt down in 976 and rebuilt two years later. In 1063 construction of yet another new church was started, modelled on the two great basilicas of Constantinople – those of the Church of the Holy Apostle (no longer in existence) and of St Sophia. Venice, having for long been the gateway between West and East, continued to

The interior of St Mark's Basilica.

maintain strong cultural links with Byzantium, and no expense was spared in the initial decoration of the basilica in Eastern rather than European style. Wealthy Venetian merchants were expected to bring treasures back from their journeys to the East, and the marbles, enamels, and precious stones, the mosaics of gold, the coloured glass, and stone *tessere* (tiles) all bore witness to the fabulous wealth of *La Serenissima*. The four magnificent bronze horses looted from Constantinople in the early thirteenth century during the Fourth Crusade were placed high on the front of St Mark's Basilica, symbolizing the freedom of Venice. Further features were added over the centuries, but although later Gothic additions lent height to the structure, the Byzantine influence continued to dominate. So overpowering is the size and shimmering beauty of the Basilica, both inside and out, that the presence of God becomes apparent even to the unbeliever.

Holding its commanding position at the head of the *piazza*, St Mark's presides over what the Emperor Napoleon described as "the finest drawing room in Europe". And it was in this drawing room that the most dramatic of the annual processions would take place – those of Holy Week, when the great and the good of Venice assembled for days of mourning, only to erupt in rejoicing on Easter Day.

The magnificence of the Basilica, scene of his first public performances as a violinist, must have inspired much of the sacred music that the Red Priest was later to write. With his father in the orchestra, St Mark's would have exerted a formative influence over his early life. Two of his great works forming part of the mass – The *Gloria* and the *Magnificat* – are filled with passion, virtuosity, and inventiveness, the instrumental music reminiscent of his concertos and the solos comparable to those of his operatic arias. The *Gloria*, composed in 1713, and the *Magnificat*, completed in 1719,

were both written for two sopranos, contralto, chorus, and orchestra, and were initially performed with their usual expertise by the girls of the Pietà. The names of the soloists from the Pietà who performed the first *Magnificat* are on record, but it has been suggested that on this particular occasion the bass parts may have been taken by males connected with the chapel, rather than transposed for the girls with deepest voices.

Three versions of the *Magnificat* and two of the *Gloria*s survive, the second *Gloria* (RV589) being regarded as the most joyful and popular of the Red Priest's sacred works. It opens in a manner that is unmistakably in the style of a Vivaldi concerto; in fact, H. C. Robbins Landon describes it as the Four Seasons of its genre. The voices of the soprano and contralto singers express a deep sense of religious emotion, their parts interspersed with the joyful singing of the chorus and the vivacity of the orchestra, which on this occasion includes the trumpet. This work would be played at the Vivaldi Week in Sienna in 1939 and was one of the first pieces of Vivaldi's church music to be recorded after the end of the Second World War. And yet not all his sacred music was in the style of his secular works, for in contrast to his more spirited religious offerings, his setting of the *Stabat Mater* (RV621), of which he and his father attended the first performance in Brescia in 1711 as part of a religious ceremony there, is a sad and sombre work, making much use of the deep contralto voice; it was to become one of his religious masterpieces.

In addition to these major offerings, Vivaldi wrote a quantity of motets, or short sacred pieces, and also provided settings for a number of psalms. Among these were the large-scale *Dixit Dominus* and *Beatus Vir*. All except possibly the latter – for which male singers would once more appear to have been indispensable – were written for initial performance by the *figlie di coro*, demonstrating yet again the exceptionally high standard achieved by the girls of the Pietà under the direction of their red-haired priest.

Singers at St Mark's were considered to be the elite, and every effort was made to prevent them from defecting to better-paid work at the opera. When celebrating major events, soprano parts would be sung by castratos and the occasional falsetto, while contraltos, tenors, and basses were divided between lay and ecclesiastical singers. They would be accompanied by anything from twenty to thirty-four instrumentalists, who were engaged for life – among them, of course, Antonio's father, Giovanni Battista Vivaldi. For daily rituals, such as the mass, vespers, and psalms, perhaps a mere dozen singers would be involved. For major festivals, as well as the soloists and orchestra there might be two main choirs, each with a large organ, situated on either side of the nave, and smaller orchestras plus organs spread along the length of the nave. When they performed together, the powerful music must have seemed to emerge magically from all four corners of the basilica.

VIVALDI AND THE ORATORIO

Between 1714 and 1716, Vivaldi was commissioned by the governing board of the Pietà to compose four oratorios, to be performed by the girls. Music for the first – *Moyses Deus Pharaonis* – has been lost, along with that of

two others. However, his masterpiece in this genre for which the music is still extant is *Juditha triumphans devicta Holofernes barbarie*, commissioned to celebrate the historic victory of the Republic of Venice over the Turks, and the regaining of the island of Corfu. As an allegory based on the struggle between the Venetians and their age-old enemies, the Turks, *Juditha triumphans* is described, in rather contradictory terms, as a sacred military work.

The plot of the oratorio revolves around an attack by the head of the Assyrian army, Holofernes (representing the Turks) on Judea (representing the Venetians). Juditha and her servant visit Holofernes' camp, ostensibly seeking peace. Holofernes falls for Juditha and dismisses his guards, the better to enjoy her company. As he relaxes, Juditha beheads him with his own sword, carrying off his head as a trophy. On her return to Judea, Juditha's triumph – that of Good over Evil – is celebrated by the chief priest of the Judeans. The libretto by Giacomo Cassetti contains captivating verse in Latin, the plot is filled with drama, and the score is lyrical.

At its first performance, the arias were sung and the parts for a wide range of solo instruments were played by the girls of the Pietà. Juditha's delicate tones were represented by the viola, chalumeau (a forerunner of the clarinet), and mandolin, while the orchestral strings symbolized the masculine Holofernes. Vivaldi, in common with other composers of the period, was never one to waste a good tune; within *Juditha triumphans* he was to incorporate elements of both the first movement of "Spring" and the country dance from The Four Seasons.

Prior to the success of this oratorio, however, there had been a temporary hitch in the Red Priest's employment at the *ospedale*: in March 1716 he was dismissed, only to be recalled some two months later. The reason is unknown, but on this occasion it is thought likely to have been an economic decision rather than as a result of further disagreement between the governors regarding his suitability. In any event, on his reinstatement, Vivaldi was given the new and rather more exalted title of *maestro dei concerti*, a position he was to hold on and off until 1739.

An oratorio, being a story on a religious or biblical theme for performance by soloists and chorus accompanied by an orchestra, but without scenery, costumes or acting, is just one step away from opera. And it was towards opera that Vivaldi next turned his attention.

Chapter 9
THE TWO FACES OF VENICE

THE POLICE STATE

Before we follow Vivaldi on his new venture into opera, it will add colour to his story if we discover a little more of the extraordinary background into which he, along with his musical contemporaries and those who had preceded him, lived and carved out their careers. For the Republic of Venice was nothing if not unusual; the city had for centuries been a place of extraordinary contrasts – and not just the contrast between land and water. Her populace combined their love of music in general and their passion for singing in particular – a passion that was well established way before Vivaldi's lifetime in the High Baroque – with the heady freedom and excesses of the Carnival. At the same time they lived under the strict regulations of a police state. It was as an escape from the rigours of governmental control, then, that they plunged so readily into the joys of Carnival and revelled in the musical and other entertainments that it offered.

The titular head of state in the Republic of Venice was the doge, though he was little more than a figurehead. In order to prevent him from becoming a dictator, his election was carried out in a convoluted manner so as to be completely immune from any form of fraud or intrigue. Although he lived in the lap of luxury, his every move was scrutinized; he could barely set one foot in front of another, let alone leave the country, without permission. The actual government lay in the hands of the *Signoria* – the Inner Council of State, whose members were drawn from the upper classes, notably those old-established Venetian families who could trace their lineage back to the first of the 120 doges in the year 709. The descendants of the twenty-four families whose names originally appeared in the Golden Book – i.e., those who had made their fortunes long since through the spoils of war or trade – still headed the hereditary ranks of the Venetian aristocracy.

Most powerful of all, however, was the Council of Ten: this body took it upon itself to appoint from among its members the Council of Three, a small, sinister, and unpopular group who formed the Inquisition in charge of security. On account of her position in Europe and her reputation as a wealthy trading nation, Venice had over the centuries become a hotbed of international espionage and intrigue, and it was well known that the many foreign embassies situated in the Republic were heavily involved in intelligence-gathering. It was government policy, therefore, to prevent the possibility of Venetian nobles becoming compromised in any way that could lead to a coup in which *La Serenissima* became a family fiefdom – as had disastrously occurred in other states of Italy. With this in mind, contact with foreigners was strictly forbidden to the upper classes; if a meeting took place, however unintentionally, it could lead to a severe punishment for the person concerned. Charles de Brosses records a noble being put to death for the sin of having been spotted as he inadvertently walked past a foreign ambassador's residence – and we have seen Vivaldi's immediate concern for his pupil Pisendel when he came under surveillance while walking with him in the Piazza San Marco. In general, then, the only way in which members of the foreign diplomatic services were able to communicate with their Venetian opposite numbers was through third parties, although, when diplomats were masked and among the crowds at the opera and at other entertainments of the Carnival season, there was opportunity for more direct, if surreptitious and potentially dangerous, communication.

Another hazard arose from the determination of the authorities to

This example of the boxes known as lions' mouths, which were placed around the city in order to facilitate the passing on of information about the Venetian inhabitants, can be seen at the Palazzo Ducale.

maintain the status quo of the Republic. If any high-ranking person was deemed to have become too popular or too full of himself, he would have to be taken down a peg or two by the authorities and in some way humiliated, in order to prevent others from following his example. An extreme case is that of a Venetian general in the fifteenth century who, having won a prolonged battle against the Turks, was charged with treason and imprisoned on his victorious return from war.

The citizens of Venice were well aware that the state kept its eye on their movements through the activities of an army of spies and informers who infiltrated all ranks of society and whose task it was to report to the government details of every kind of inappropriate behaviour. Indeed, to facilitate the passing on of information by all and sundry, boxes known as *bocche di*

DENONTIE SECRETE
CONTRO CHI OCCVLTERA
GRATIE ET OFFICII,
Ō COLLVDERA PER
NASCONDER LA VERA
RENDITA D ESSI

leone (lions' mouths) were placed around the city, into which anyone could post a denunciation. Had CCTV been invented, it would doubtless have been a welcome addition to the armoury of the government. And so it was a very real fear of punishment that could include torture or summary execution that kept the populace from causing trouble. By the time of Vivaldi's birth, there had been some considerable relaxation of the rules and restrictions of earlier centuries, although we have seen the fairly stiff sentences handed down to his brothers. And it is on record that between 1741 and 1762 the extraordinarily large number of 73,000 people were either executed or committed to the galleys for life. Indeed, anyone deemed to be disturbing the public order could be put to death without question.

HALF A YEAR OF HEDONISM

Carnival came as a total contrast to these extremes of governmental control. The year was more or less divided in half and the two periods could not have been more different. From Easter to October, relative sobriety reigned. Ordinary citizens went about their business as normal, male members of the nobility soberly clad in black without any adornment, although on festive occasions the young men dressed in the latest brilliant fashions. Come Carnival, however, conformity went out of the window – not only conformity, but also class distinction, for the delights were not just for the privileged few but for the pleasure of all. During this time the upper classes, who normally kept their distance from the *cittadini* (citizens) and the *popolani* (plebeians), were able to mingle on equal terms with people at all levels of society. It was almost as though Venice herself was bipolar, oscillating manically between austerity and hedonism, pain and pleasure, dark and light.

It was almost as though Venice herself was bipolar, oscillating manically between austerity and hedonism, pain and pleasure, dark and light.

The period of Carnival expanded until it virtually overlapped the autumn operatic season, which began each year on the first Sunday in October, continuing until two weeks before Christmas. After a brief respite for the religious celebrations, Carnival proper started up on 26 December and carried on feverishly until Shrove Tuesday, whereupon everything stopped once more for the period of Lent. But this was not the end, for there were two further weeks of frenetic revelry after the Feast of the Ascension before the season was finally over.

One of the most spectacular celebrations was the Ascension Day "Marriage with the Sea". This colourful event took place in commemoration of the victory by the Lombard League of northern Italian cities (including the Republic of Venice) over the Holy Roman Emperor Frederick Barbarossa in 1177. In Vivaldi's lifetime it also served as a reminder of the Republic's once far-reaching sea power. On this day the doge, the papal nuncio, ambassadors, and other important guests, were rowed out to sea in the *Bucintoro* – an extravagantly carved, gilded, and decorated barge, double-decked, and manned by a choir of 168 oarsmen. On reaching the waters of the Adriatic beyond the Lido, the doge would throw a wedding ring into the sea, proclaiming: "We wed thee, O Sea, as a sign of true and perpetual dominion." Then came the approving roar of artillery fire and the cheers of the thousands of Venetians who had followed the maritime procession in small boats. On his return to dry land, and after having heard mass at San Nicolo on the Lido, the doge would give a vast banquet of thirty courses for the nobles and distinguished guests, the general public being invited to participate in the first course. A fair was set up on the Piazza San Marco, to the delight of the Venetians, who were able to indulge themselves in a further couple of weeks of licensed pleasure. And music, of course, played an important part throughout the celebrations.

During the Carnival season, people of all classes dressed in exotic costumes and it was *de rigueur* always to wear a mask. Indeed, the nobles were required to wear masks year round when out in society – attending theatres, casinos, or other places of leisure – in order both to indicate their social rank and also to maintain their anonymity; failure to do so could invoke the strong arm of the law. Some masks covered the whole face, enabling the wearer completely to conceal his or her identity; others more elegantly covered the upper face only, allowing the wearer to eat, drink, and talk with ease. Masks with a hawk-like beaked nose were popular, as was the white-painted full-face mask worn with a black cloak. Some masks enhanced beauty; some were positively sinister. Such was the demand

that Venice boasted a guild of *mascherari* (mask-makers), whose members created confections in papier mâché, black velvet, waxed cloth, or leather, some topped with a veil, some a ghostly white, others decorated with painted designs. It was this love of disguise that enabled the normally sober citizenry to throw off the shackles of conformity and indulge in whatever outrageous behaviour they chose, without fear of recognition. Indeed, to add further to the confusion, some concealed themselves in black cloaks or priests' robes, while others cross-dressed.

Throughout this joyful chaos, however, there was no let-up in the activities of the spies and informers, for Carnival or no Carnival, the government never ceased to maintain its policy of surveillance. And, of course, not only did the masks and disguises enable the pickpockets and ne'er-do-wells to go about their business amid the revelling crowds, but they also provided ample opportunity for the spies, similarly masked, to listen in to conversations and check up on the activities of the citizens undetected. Whether Vivaldi participated in the round of Carnival partying, or whether he was fully engaged in providing musical entertainment for the revellers, is unfortunately unrecorded.

So Carnival was a time when nobles could mix with commoners, when contact could be made between people who would not normally communicate with one another, and in particular a time when flirtations and affairs could flourish behind a mask – for Venice had the reputation of being the capital city of sensuality. Aristocratic women bleached their hair and indulged in their love of rich clothes and jewels, wearing low-cut gowns and tottering about on ridiculously tall clogs – useful at times of *aqua alta* (high water) but highly dangerous on dry land. Venetian women had a reputation for being both beautiful and flirtatious, a beauty spot placed near the eye indicating that the wearer was irresistible, or, perhaps more accurately, unlikely to resist. Aristocratic women in general were not supposed to wear jewellery at all, apart from during the first two years of marriage, when pearls presented by their mothers-in-law were permitted – although, as women will, they tended to find ways around this unpopular diktat.

During Carnival, people dined out, danced, and attended theatres, concerts, and the opera – activities for which they had an inexhaustible appetite and that provided months of welcome work for composers, singers, and musicians. Additionally, Venetians indulged in their addiction to gambling at the gaming tables of the famous Ridotto and other, less prestigious, casinos. As well as their entertainment value, these various venues provided society with places to meet and carry on their romantic affairs. There were plenty of outdoor enjoyments too: battles between the inhabitants of the different *sestieri*, fist fights on the bridges, and bull-baiting. Diarist John Evelyn, who attended what he described as the "universal madness" of Carnival, also referred to "a barbarous custom of hunting bulls about the streets and piazzas, which is very dangerous", after which the beasts would finally be despatched by the sword. Evelyn also records the somewhat unpleasant fact that "during Carnival they fling eggs filled with sweet water, but sometimes not over-sweet". Then there were the fortune-tellers, jugglers, acrobatic dancers, and high stilt walkers – and everywhere, of course, street music.

Although it may seem as if Carnival contravened the austere principles of the government, it was in fact in the authorities' interest that it should

Here, Pietro Longhi's masked figures are seen in the *Ridotto* (gaming rooms).

thrive. For not only did it keep the populace in this strictly regulated Republic happy (enabling the young men to use up energies which might otherwise have been employed in less desirable activities, such as rioting), but it also attracted vast numbers of visitors, who spent small fortunes that made a valuable contribution to the coffers of the state. During Carnival, Venice acted as a magnet for music-lovers, attracting the nobility from all over Europe to join in the revels and to visit the opera. Indeed, one opera buff – Prince Charles Albert of Bavaria – is said to have attended four operas in three days. And although the normal population of Venice at the beginning of the eighteenth century was around 160,000, that figure was swelled by some 30,000 visitors during the period of Carnival.

THE PURSUIT OF PLEASURE

Part of this invasion consisted of armies of courtesans who arrived from other parts of Italy and from all over Europe to join the Venetian prostitutes. These women ranged from upper-class beauties to simple country girls hoping to earn a living, and their services were offered more or less openly throughout the city. In the sixteenth century, prostitutes were confined to a red-light district and strictly supervised – indeed, what else could be expected in a city whose regulations covered pretty well every activity? Some, however, were elegant, refined, cultivated, and much sought after by the nobility. But it was not only the courtesans – described by English traveller Thomas Coryate as "these amorous calypsos" – who benefited from the licentious climate of Carnival. During the first year of marriage, aristocratic ladies behaved as one might expect; after that time they were free to go out and about without

Portrait of the English poet George Gordon, Lord Byron, who commented on the social aspect of Venice. This portrait is after an original painting by Thomas Phillips.

their husbands – who were in any case probably amusing themselves elsewhere. It was quite common for a young wife to acquire an aristocratic young male companion – a *cicisbeo* – who might or might not be a lover, but who would accompany her on her social rounds, and who would not necessarily be disapproved of by her husband. Indeed, sometimes the three of them would go about together. Lord Byron remarked that a woman who limited herself to her husband and one lover was virtuous, while those who had two, three, or more were just a little wild. Shakespeare too picked up on the reputation of these wild women in his *Othello*: "In Venice they do let heaven see the pranks they dare not show their husbands; their best conscience is not to leave't undone, but keep't unknown."

The wearing of masks, of course, facilitated the "keeping unknown" of the amorous adventures of both sexes, which were legendary. The infamous Casanova, who was born in Venice in 1725 and whose name perhaps more than any other conjures up images of debauchery, was convicted in 1755 of black magic and freemasonry and sentenced to imprisonment for a year in the attic cells at the top of the doge's palace. With the help of a fellow prisoner he managed to escape by climbing on to the leaded roof and sliding down to the floor beneath, where he convinced an official that he was a guest who had been inadvertently locked in. Once freed, the libertine made his departure to the safety of France, where he remained in exile for many years.

Back in Venice, however, when the Carnival season was finally over, after such a prolonged period of frenzied indulgence it is likely that most citizens were in fact quite glad to have the occasional early night.

Chapter 10
OPERA

Claudio Monteverdi (c. 1567–1643), whose *Orfeo* marked a major advance in the development of opera.

THE VENETIAN PASSION

As we saw in the previous chapter, Venice more than any other city of its time was created for pleasure of every kind. And one of the greatest and most widely enjoyed pleasures was opera. From the beginning of the seventeenth century, opera in one form or another had spread throughout Italy, attracting not just the elite but people of all classes. In the late sixteenth century the Camerata of Florence (a group of academics who gathered together to discuss both the arts and the sciences) had attempted to revive Greek drama, in which, they believed, music and poetry had been combined, with an emphasis on the declamation of the text. It was from this notion that polyphony was replaced by a single melodic line with continuo accompaniment, leading to the recitative that provided the foundation for the new musical concept. Transformed by the composer Monteverdi when he presented his ground-breaking opera *Orfeo* in Mantua in 1607, this new

spectacle was taken up with enthusiasm by other Italian cities, notably Naples and Rome, where lavish performances were given at the court of Pope Urban VIII. The Venetians, of course, with their passion for music, were quick to seize on the novel form of entertainment, opening the San Cassiano theatre expressly for the purpose. In 1613 Monteverdi, having been responsible for initiating the opera as we know it, was appointed to the prestigious position of *maestro di capella* at St Mark's

Pietro Metastasio (1698–1782),
dramatist, whose libretti were set
to music by virtually all the major
composers of his day, including Vivaldi.

PIETRO METASTASIO
ROMANO POETA CESAREO

Basilica in Venice. Here he remained for the rest of his life, composing both religious and secular music, along with further operatic works.

In its early days, opera comprised a harmonious union of words and music. As time progressed, it developed a set format that included lengthy recitatives that narrated the plot, and arias designed to show off the talents of the singers. As the operatic aria became increasingly dramatic, the singer, in order to give greater emphasis to the meaning of the words and to express more clearly the emotions they engendered, began to take liberties with the music. Thus the profile of the singer came to the fore – leading to the cult of personality and the celebration of the diva and the castrato. For a considerable time there was operatic rivalry between Venice and Naples, leading to many of the best Venetian singers being poached from the superb choir of St Mark's in order to meet the ever-increasing demand for this secular form of entertainment. Towards the end of the seventeenth century, however, Venetian operatic domination started to fade with the arrival of an increasing number of Neapolitan singers who were treated as superstars and whose fame spread throughout Europe.

There were two genres of opera in Italy in the eighteenth century. The *dramma di musica* or *opera seria* was for and about the nobility. Based on mythical, classical, or heroic subjects in which virtue was shown to be rewarded, this operatic style was heavily influenced by the libretti of the poet Metastasio. Naples was a centre for the development of *opera seria*, and here pride of place was given to the high voices of the renowned castrati; there was little room for the bass in *opera seria*. The operatic format generally comprised a three-movement overture followed by recitatives, interspersed by a series of florid arias. All the leading singers expected their fair share of the limelight, and it was the task of the librettist and the composer to ensure that sufficient numbers of arias were allotted to the singers in proportion to their status.

Opera buffa or *opera comico*, by contrast, with its small cast and modest staging, was light-hearted opera for the common man, featuring everyday settings and subjects, simple words, local dialect, and clear diction; a couple of comic interludes would be thrown in during the intervals between the acts, and the whole performance bore a distinct resemblance to the *commedia dell'arte* of the sixteenth and seventeenth centuries. It was in *opera buffa* that the *basso buffo*, or bass singer, came into his own as the central or comic character. The light operas of Mozart, Puccini, and Rossini derive from this genre.

Resembling a short oratorio or a mini opera, the cantata had no scenery or action, thus being similar in presentation to the oratorio; at the same time, in parallel with the operatic aria, the solo voice grew in importance. As in the case of the sonata mentioned above, there were two forms: the *cantata da camera* (chamber cantata), based on a secular subject, and the *cantata da chiesa* (church cantata), bearing a sacred theme. Although originating in Italy – Vivaldi was to write numerous sacred cantatas – the genre developed in different ways in other countries, its popularity later spreading, with the rediscovery of Bach's music, to Germany and England.

In the seventeenth and eighteenth centuries, spending a night at the opera in one of the commercial theatres of Venice was a very different experience from taking a seat in the hallowed atmosphere of the opera house of modern times. The prestigious Teatro San Cassiano was a meeting place for people from all walks of life, the nobility masked as usual. In the

> *Members of the audience were given to playing chess to relieve the boredom of the lengthy recitatives, not to mention dropping orange peel and apple cores, and even spitting on to the heads of the people below...*

opera houses, people could gather round the gaming tables to play cards, eat, drink, smoke, chat – and from time to time watch the performance. What is more, having taken opera as an entertainment to their hearts, the Venetians did not hesitate to make known their approbation or disapproval of the singers and the works on offer, frequently in a rowdy manner. Members of the audience were given to playing chess to relieve the boredom of the lengthy recitatives, not to mention dropping orange peel and apple cores, and even spitting on to the heads of the people below, a habit that encouraged those who could afford it to pay for the safety of a box. Vivaldi's friend Uffenbach, who in his inexperience had taken a seat in the parterre during Carnival, was amazed to discover members of the audience smoking, gambling, and playing chess during the performance – and even more astounded to find a gob of spit from above landing on his libretto. Boxes were popular for reasons other than protection: often hired by the nobles and wealthy members of society for the season and treated like private drawing rooms, they provided a venue both for parties and for amorous liaisons. It was customary for an opera to last from seven until eleven in the evening, after which the Venetians – whose appetite for pleasure appears to have been insatiable – were quite likely to proceed to a ball.

A large number of theatres sprang up in the Republic to satisfy the obsession with *dramma di musica* – more, it is said than anywhere else in Europe. When it is appreciated that 432 operas were performed in Venice in the first half of the eighteenth century, this figure does not seem excessive. As many as sixteen theatres came and went during the seventeenth century alone – the most popular, the San Cassiano, owned by the Tron family, was

*A night at the
opera was indeed
an event to
remember!*

both first and last, staying the course until the end of the Republic, while the Vendramins' San Luca lasted just three years. Other notable patrician proprietors included the Grimanis, owners of Santi Giovanni e Paolo, San Giovanni Grisostomo, and San Samuele; the Guistinians of San Moise; and the Marcellos and Capellos of Sant'Angelo, the latter playing an important role in Vivaldi's operatic career. The better funded the theatre, the better the quality of singers that could be afforded, and the more magnificent the presentation. Huge machines were devised by an ex-naval engineer from the Arsenal, Giacomo Torelli. It was his skills that enabled the theatres to install and operate elaborate scene changes, mechanical animals such as camels and elephants, flying machines, and a stage that revolved by means of a complicated collection of winches and pulleys, ropes, and sails. Live horses also made their appearance – an unusual sight in a Venice where horses were a rarity. A night at the opera was indeed an event to remember!

THE RED PRIEST AT THE OPERA

In 1713 Vivaldi determined to launch himself into this glamorous world. Having been given a month's leave from the Pietà, he was to stage his first opera, *Ottone in Villa* (with a libretto by Domenico Lalli) in Vicenza. It was the habit of Venetians to abandon the capital during the summer, passing their holidays in provincial centres on the Terrafirma or Veneto, as Venetian mainland possessions were known. Vivaldi's nervousness about his opera's reception may explain its unveiling in Vicenza during the summer exodus, rather than in Venice itself. However, his fears were unfounded, giving him sufficient confidence to choose Venice for his next production. Indeed, 1714

A London reprint of
Vivaldi's Opus IV *La
Stravaganza*, dating from
around 1740.

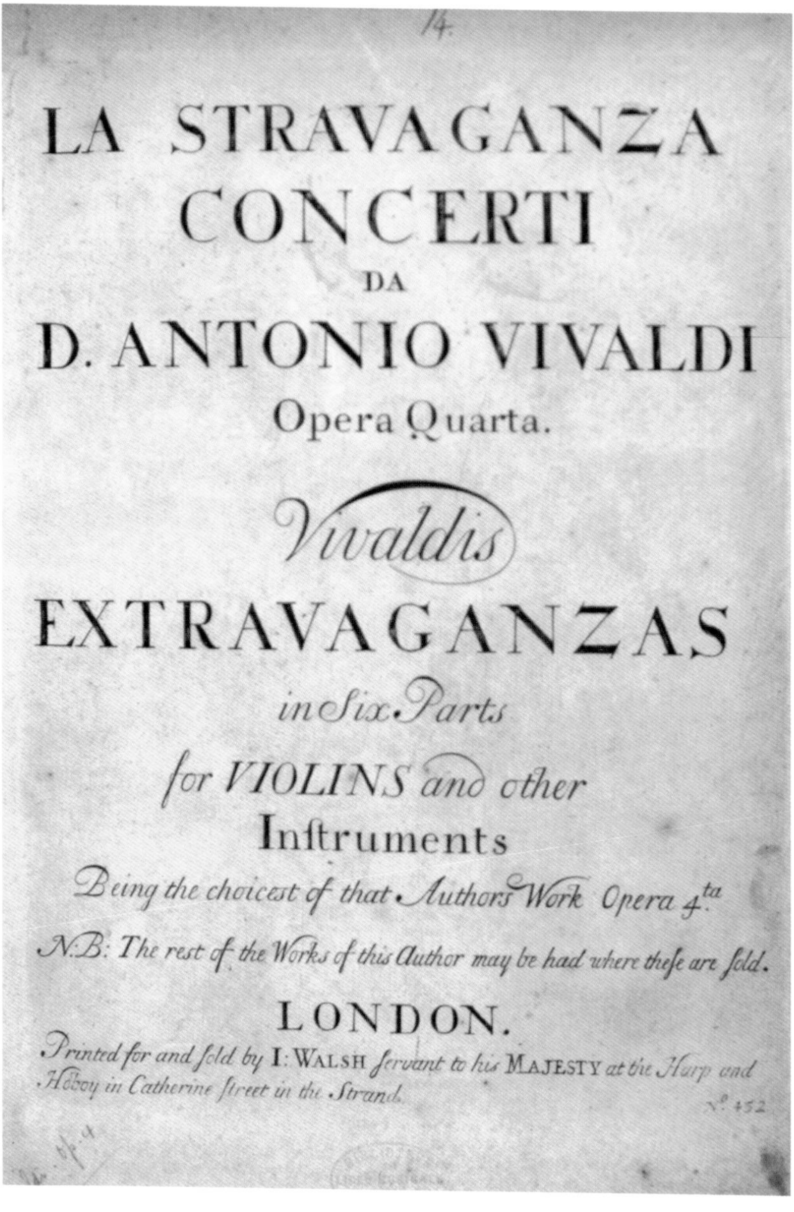

14.

LA STRAVAGANZA
CONCERTI
DA
D. ANTONIO VIVALDI
Opera Quarta.

Vivaldis

EXTRAVAGANZAS
in Six Parts
for VIOLINS and other
Instruments

Being the choicest of that Authors Work Opera 4.ᵗᵃ

N:B: The rest of the Works of this Author may be had where these are sold.

LONDON.

*Printed for and sold by I: WALSH servant to his MAJESTY at the Harp and
Hoboy in Catherine street in the Strand.*

Nᵒ 452

The scenery and lighting of the
Teatro di San Samuele is depicted in
this eighteenth-century painting by
Gabriel Bella.

was to prove a particularly rewarding year on two fronts, for not only was he to present for the first time an opera in Venice but he was also to receive high praise for his newly published Opus 4 – *La Stravaganza*.

Despite his growing success, however, Vivaldi continued to feel himself snubbed by the nobles on account of his plebeian background. This state of affairs both infuriated him and added to the determination with which he pursued his operatic career, for that was where both Vivaldis saw fame and fortune. It so happened that Antonio's father had had a connection with the Teatro Sant'Angelo, one of the smaller theatres in the San Marco *sestiere*, although the exact nature of this involvement is unclear. However, a document dated March 1710 lists Giovanni Battista Vivaldi among its creditors. It was to this theatre that the Vivaldis, father and son, turned their attention.

The land on which the Teatro Sant'Angelo had been built by impresario

Francesco Saturini was owned by the patrician Capello and Marcello families. Legal wrangles in connection with land tenure had led to bad feeling, some of which would later seem to have rubbed off on to Antonio Vivaldi and his father, who were to have considerable involvement with the management of the theatre over a period of years, Antonio acting as composer and impresario and Giambattista playing the violin. It was here in 1714 that Vivaldi's second operatic venture, *Orlando Finto Pazzo*, based on Grazio Braccioli's libretto, was performed. It was not initially well received and was replaced after a couple of weeks by a work given the previous year. This was followed in 1715 by *Nerone fatto Cesare*, with music by seven different composers and a libretto by Matteo Noris, for which Vivaldi wrote eleven arias. This patchwork procedure was not unusual: many operatic productions were *pasticcios* (paste-ups of bits and pieces from previous productions and/or by more than one composer). Vivaldi – never one to miss an opportunity for a bit of boasting – claimed to have written ninety-eight operas; however, a figure below fifty appears more realistic, any others more than likely to have been revisions or pasticcios.

As we have seen, most operas in the Baroque era were based on historical or mythological plots, the more dramatic the better – although the libretto had to meet with the approval of the censor. Vivaldi's next offering, *Arsilda Regina di Ponto* (another collaboration with librettist Domenico Lalli), initially failed on this account, since the heroine committed the sin of falling in love with another woman, albeit one disguised as a man. It was passed the following year, however, and became a resounding success. Vivaldi was to base his operas on libretti from a number of different sources. Rarely able to afford the most fashionable, he tended to use works by lesser-known writers or to revive old libretti. He did, however, base three operas on libretti by the famous poet Metastasio – *Siroe, Re de Persia, L'Olimpiade,* and *Catone in Utica* – and six on libretti by Domenico Lalli.

The Red Priest's involvement with the Teatro Sant'Angelo continued. In 1716 he wrote two further musical dramas – *L'Incoronazione di Dario* and *La Constanza Trionfante degli Amori e degli Odi,* the former based on a libretto by Adriano Morsello and the latter by Antonio Marchi – and he was to go on to compose a total of eighteen operas for the theatre, taking on the demanding role of impresario for many of them. It was normally the custom for the proprietors or directors of a theatre to appoint an impresario to handle the business side of affairs. This individual would be responsible for deciding the repertoire for the season, negotiating with the composers and librettists, auditioning singers and engaging instrumentalists, organizing scenery and costume designers, dealing with promotion and ticket sales – and risking his own money on the enterprise into the bargain. It was a chancy investment: if the opera was a success, he could make a good profit; if a failure, he could be bankrupted. In Vivaldi's case, the pressure was increased by his often taking on the additional tasks of composer and instrumentalist. Although the Vivaldis were unable to afford elaborate scenery or the best singers – the divas and the celebrated castrati from Naples who wowed the audiences at the richer theatres – nevertheless seats at the Sant'Angelo had the advantage of being cheaper, thus attracting those who could not afford to patronize the more distinguished opera houses. Vivaldi tended to convince himself that any venture in which he was involved would be a success, and it must therefore have been gratifying to him to know that Uffenbach, for one, claimed that the singers at the Sant'Angelo were every bit as good as those of the big opera houses.

At the same time that he was breaking into the operatic world, Vivaldi was also receiving public acclaim for his oratorio *Juditha triumphans*. Its performance by the girls of the Pietà became a must on the wish list of visitors to Venice, who could then complete their enjoyment with a night at the Teatro Sant'Angelo, where the Red Priest himself would on occasion dazzle the audience by playing his violin in a manner virtuosic and incredibly fast. Despite his many other commitments, Vivaldi also managed to maintain at least some of his obligations to the *ospedale* during this time, although there is no mention of him in the Pietà records between the years 1719 and 1722.

Composing, playing, conducting, and private teaching, not to mention taking on the many duties of impresario – such a workload would be taxing for a man in the best of health; for someone disabled by a permanent "tightness in the chest" it seems little short of miraculous. Nevertheless, there was to be no respite, for following his undeniable initial successes in both opera and oratorio, even the Venetians were beginning to sit up and take notice – and more importantly, doors were to start opening for him further afield.

Chapter 11
THE MANTUA YEARS

THE CAPELLMEISTER

Although his instrumental and sacred works had been well received in Venice, in the world of *dramma di musica* the Red Priest was finding himself up against stiff competition from his many contemporaries. He was in something of a catch-22 situation: being unable to afford to hire theatres of the first rank that could give a major boost to his reputation and income, he was confined to second-class theatres such as the Sant'Angelo or the San Samuele, which did neither. It became clear to both father and son that if Antonio were to achieve the level of fame and wealth in this genre that he craved and felt he deserved, he would have to look to other European countries where he was already becoming well known for his instrumental works. And he spent much of the rest of his life doing just that.

His travels began early in 1718, when he took up the position of *maestro di cappella da camera*, or chamber capellmeister, at the court of Prince Philip of Hesse-Darmstadt in Mantua. Bordering on the Veneto, Mantua had been a centre of the arts in the seventeenth century, and had always had a strong link with the musical world of Venice. At one time, under the rule of the dukes of Gonzaga, Mantua had latterly become a fief of the Austrian empire. Prince Philip (the "Landgrave", to give him his Austrian title), being aware of Vivaldi's work both as player and composer, decided to invite the flamboyant Venetian to his court in order to give a shot in the arm to the cultural life of the principality. For Vivaldi himself, the offer arrived at exactly the right moment; it presented an opportunity to take a break from the Pietà and from Venetian society, and to move to a city where he hoped to be appreciated for his achievements rather than relegated, as he saw it, to the second rank on account of his plebeian background.

Mantua, capital of the province of the same name, was situated in Lombardy. It bore a watery similarity to Venice in that it was surrounded on three sides by artificial lakes that had been created in the twelfth century from the waters of the River Mincio that flowed from Lake Garda. Thought to have been founded on marshy land around 2000 BC by the Etruscans, the city had been conquered over the centuries by the Romans, the Byzantines, the Franks, and the Lombards, passing through the hands of a series of rulers, the last of whom was Countess Matilda of Canossa. After her death in 1115, the city became a free commune, distancing itself from the Holy Roman Empire. Later, Mantua joined the Lombard League; when Vivaldi made his entrance to the city, it was under Austrian rule.

During his years in Mantua, Vivaldi produced chamber cantatas and serenatas for the court. The cantata, being a popular vocal form generally written for solo voice with harpsichord or cello accompaniment, was particularly favoured by singers seeking work outside the opera season. Vivaldi's cantatas showed a marked contrast between the flowing idiom of the voice and the accompaniment (which could sometimes comprise several instruments). The chamber cantata was a secular work with the setting invariably an Arcadian landscape inhabited by nymphs and shepherds, the recitative generally in the form of a monologue by the singer. Thirty solo cantatas by Vivaldi are preserved in the Foà and Giordano collections in Turin (along with many of his other works). Of these, twenty-two were for soprano and eight for alto; they follow his three-movement format – recitative, aria, recitative – as opposed to the

Fifteenth-century fresco painting of the Piazza Broletto in Mantua.

four-movement format preferred by Albinoni, his prolific contemporary in this field.

Serenatas, or serenades, to commemorate important events at court were much in demand in countries other than Venice – which, being a republic, of course, had no court. This did not stop ambassadors to Venice from frequently commissioning serenatas to celebrate royal weddings, the birthdays of their monarchs, or other significant occasions. Often performed at night, either at court or in the gardens of the *palazzo* of an aristocrat, the subject matter of a serenata would be allegorical, mythological, or pastoral, its characters' prime purpose being to heap praise upon the recipient. With up to six singers, the form of a serenata could be described as being somewhere between a cantata and an opera.

While in Mantua, Vivaldi devoted much of his energy to composing music for opera, including *Teuzzone* (set in China), *La Candace*, and *Tito Manlio* (libretto by Matteo Noris again). He claimed to have written the latter in just five days (his autograph score is proudly inscribed "*Musica del Vivaldi fatta in 5 giorni*") for the forthcoming marriage of Prince Philip to the widowed Princess Eleanora of Guastalla. The opera may have been completed on time, but the princess called off the wedding. However, it being Carnival season, the prince decided to go ahead with some of the planned celebrations for the non-event, among them the premiere of *Tito Manlio*, which proved a financial success for its composer.

As we have seen, opera in the Baroque age followed a set format that included lengthy recitatives and arias especially designed to show off the talents of the singers. Dramatist Carlo Goldoni, who was to write a number of libretti for Vivaldi's operas, relates being instructed to provide for five arias for the three main characters, three for the second male lead, and just one or two for the lesser characters. The librettist additionally had to take into account the size of the stage, the scenery changes, the style of the costumes, and any other demands of the impresario. Of prime importance was the amount of cash that would be available for the production. The composer seems to have come last in the line, being paid considerably less than some of the singers. The proliferation of new operas, therefore, was necessary not only to feed the demanding appetite of the public, but also to provide an income for the composer. With this in mind, Vivaldi was coming up with at least a couple a year. His operas, however, although most did well enough, were not to prove the money-spinners that he had hoped, partly because in the operatic world he was one among many, and perhaps also because his operas failed to weave quite the same magic as his instrumental works.

While in Mantua, the Red Priest was also supervising production of his operas elsewhere, in 1718 taking off for Florence, where he had been invited to provide a work for the reopening of the Florentine Teatro della Pergola. For this event he came up with librettist Antonio Salvi's *Scanderbeg*, the tale of an Albanian prince who led a successful rebellion against the Turks, a theme bearing a certain resemblance to that of his popular oratorio *Juditha triumphans*. A further example, one might say, of Vivaldi's recycling habit.

LA GIRO

Music, however, was not the only major event in Vivaldi's life that occurred in Mantua, for it was here that he made the acquaintance of the sisters

Paolina and Anna Giraud (or Giro, to give the Italianized version of the surname, by which they became known). Anna is said by Carlo Goldoni to have been born in Venice, the daughter of a French coiffeur and wig-maker – a social background not dissimilar to that of Antonio Vivaldi. However, she is believed to have been brought up in Mantua, and accordingly was sometimes known as Anna Mantovana. She was said to be small, graceful and charming, with beautiful eyes and an enchanting mouth, although her mezzo soprano voice was not strong. Fortunately, in Baroque opera, a voice of clarity and purity was of prime importance, in contrast to the powerful delivery required of the modern diva. And Anna was a gifted actress, a talent that was to make up, at least in Vivaldi's eyes, for any vocal deficiencies she might have had.

She was apparently a youngster in the care of her elder sister, Paolina, when Vivaldi first encountered the two of them – or was that really the first occasion? For it is hinted by some that Anna may have been one of the Red Priest's pupils at the Pietà, among whom there was known to have been a talented and favoured "Annina". So did their first meeting take place in Venice or in Mantua? And was their relationship one of teacher and pupil? Or priest and mistress? Or even, as suggested by Italian musicologist Gabriele Fantoni, man and wife? It would seem unlikely that the "Annina" of the Pietà would have become a professional opera singer, a commercial career being rare for those who had formed part of the *figlie di coro*, unless she had been a paying pupil. And for a high-profile priest, even if not a practising one, to take a mistress (still less a wife) would very likely have stirred up investigations by the Venetian Inquisition – and there is no record of any such happening. Although it was not uncommon for monks and priests to form relationships with women – often nuns – for someone as much in the public eye as the Red Priest it would have been an unwise move, and Vivaldi himself was vehemently to deny any wrongdoing. Nevertheless, biographer Michael Talbot suggests that Vivaldi, by putting himself in a potentially scandalous situation, would at least have expected to enjoy some of the benefits. And bearing in mind the fact that *il Prete Rosso* was never one to conform, it is perfectly possible that he followed his heart in love as in music. Whatever the situation, gossip simmered beneath the surface, and Anna Giro became widely known as "*l'Annina del Prete Rosso*". Despite the speculation regarding the relationship between the priest and the singer, however, no final conclusion has ever been reached. What is certain is that their relationship, whatever it may have been, was to have a less than benign influence on certain events in the future.

Of course, it may simply be that Antonio, having discovered the young singer in Mantua, took her on as his pupil and protégée and, as her voice developed, made her the star of many of his operatic productions. As for Paolina, it is suggested that she continued to act as chaperone to her younger sister while also becoming secretary-cum-housekeeper and/ or nurse to the often ailing priest. Whatever the circumstances, it would seem that when the two women met Vivaldi in Mantua, they seized the opportunity for Anna to further her career as a singer, at the same time doubtless only too delighted to be brought under the financial umbrella of the Red Priest.

In 1720, however, Vivaldi's spell in Mantua came to an abrupt halt with the closure of all theatres on the death of the Empress Eleonore Magdalena Theresa. It was time to return to Venice.

Chapter 12
ON THE ROAD

IL TEATRO ALLA MODA

Up to this point it seems likely that, when in Venice, Vivaldi had continued to live in the family house. Certainly his father had always played an important role in Antonio's life, travelling with him, advising him on musical matters, acting as copyist, and helping with the administration of the theatres – not to mention keeping an eye on his health. With the arrival of the Giro sisters in Venice, however, change was in the air. Whether the two women joined the Vivaldi family household, or whether they lived in separate accommodation provided by the Red Priest for the use of his protégées, is the subject of speculation. However, years later, when accused of sexual misdemeanours in connection with the sisters, Vivaldi insisted that no matter what the gossips might say, he had a house of his own and another, *a long way away*, for the Giros. In the circumstances, he would hardly say otherwise. One can only wonder, along with Hamlet, whether he did not perhaps protest too much. Whatever the truth of the matter, he got away with it – until Ferrara.

Vivaldi is next recorded as being back at the helm of the Teatro Sant'Angelo in order to stage his new opera, *La Verità in Cimento* (with a libretto by Giovanni Palazzo). But here he was hit by an untimely and entirely unexpected blow. His flamboyant operatic style and autocratic manner had disturbed some of the more conventional musicians in the city, among them Benedetto Marcello. A member of one of the two patrician families who had fought and lost a legal case against the Sant'Angelo theatre management, Benedetto was a magistrate and an amateur composer of some distinction, being particularly well known for his cantatas for solo voice and for his settings for a collection of psalms. He seems also to have

Benedetto Marcello's satirical pamphlet criticizing the artificiality of Italian *opera seria*.

IL
TEATRO
ALLA MODA

O SIA

METODO ſicuro, e facile per ben comporre, & eſequire
l'OPERE Italiane in Muſica all'uſo moderno,

Nel quale

Si danno Avvertimenti utili , e neceſſarij à Poeti, Compoſitori
di Muſica , Muſici dell'uno , e dell'altro ſeſſo , Impreſarj,
Suonatori, Ingegneri , e Pittori di Scene, Parti buffe,
Sarti , Paggi , Comparſe , Suggeritori , Copiſti,
Protettori , e MADRI di Virtuoſe , & altre
Perſone appartenenti al Teatro.

DEDICATO

DALL' AUTTORE DEL LIBRO
AL COMPOSITORE DI ESSO

Stampato ne BORGHI di BELISANIA per ALDIVIVA
LICANTE , all' Inſegna dell'ORSO in PEATA
Si vende nella STRADA del CORALLO alla
PORTA del PALAZZO d'ORLANDO.

E ſi riſtamperà ogn'anno con nuova aggiunta

been a man bearing a particular grudge against the Red Priest, partly no doubt on account of the plebeian Vivaldis having become involved in the running of the patrician Marcellos' theatre. In December 1720 Benedetto wrote, supposedly anonymously, a satire entitled *Il Teatro alla Moda* (The Fashionable Theatre). This was to all intents and purposes intended as a compendium of hints to everyone in any way connected with the world of opera including composers, singers, designers, and even patrons. Clever it may have been, but as a result it is for his bitter satirical comments rather than for his musical achievements that Benedetto is remembered.

Illustrated on the front of the pamphlet was a rowing boat, representing the theatre, with a small angel playing a violin at the back, one foot on the rudder, one keeping time, indicating a musician and entrepreneur. Seated in the boat was a large figure at the oars intended to portray Modotto, then impresario of the Sant'Angelo, and a bear depicting Orsato, impresario of the San Samuele, where Vivaldi's operas had also been performed. The pamphlet jibed at pretty well everyone connected with the theatre, in particular the castrato, who "will sing on stage with his mouth half-closed, his teeth clenched; in short he will do his utmost to prevent anyone from understanding a single word of what he's uttering", and the modern woman singer who "will always be late for rehearsals", will moan about her stage costume, "which is a poor design and isn't fashionable", and will constantly demand changes to her part. The pamphlet also attacked the scenery, the librettists, and the rest of the singers in general. However, by means of a series of anagrams, puns, and *double entendres*, it would seem to have reserved its sharpest barbs for Vivaldi, even giving "Aldiviva" – a blazingly obvious anagram of A. Vivaldi – as the name of the printer.

Whatever the intended purpose of the pamphlet, its jibes certainly did Antonio no good at all, for following its appearance, none of his operas appeared at the Sant'Angelo for the next four years. It was an opportune moment for him to resume his travels.

A PROPHET IS NOT WITHOUT HONOUR...

Milan was the first port of call, for a performance of his opera *La Silvia* as a celebration on the occasion of the birthday of the Empress Elisabeth. This work does not appear to have received any great acclaim, although it was followed by a successful oratorio of which unfortunately only the libretto survives, the music having been lost. Next came Turin, where he was commissioned to write a serenata, which was said to be a "most beautiful serenade with violins and oboes", in honour of the Princess of Sulzbach's wedding in March 1722.

And then to Rome, where his visit was described as "a social and professional triumph". Queen Christina of Sweden, who on her abdication had moved to Rome, was the driving force behind the musical life of the city, organizing starry events at her residence at the *palazzo* Riario. Composers of such repute as Corelli, Scarlatti, and later Handel all worked for a time in the eternal city, benefiting from its cultural climate. Vivaldi's "Lombard style" (a rhythmic system of "reversed dotting" and also known as the Scotch Snap) went down particularly well in Rome. Quantz, who had first heard Vivaldi's works in 1714, encountered the Red Priest ten years later in Rome, where he commented that the Romans were so captivated by the Lombard style that they were unable to endure anything that "was not conceived in that style".

Rome, the Eternal City, scene of
Vivaldi's 'social and professional
triumph'.

Vivaldi was to receive a further unexpected boost to his career and
his social standing when his ex-pupil Alessandro Marcello, brother of the
embittered Benedetto, wrote to Princess Maria Livia Spinola Borghese,
suggesting that she extend her protection to "Dom Antonio Vivaldi, professor
and violin player". Was this an apology for his brother's behaviour? If so,
it was a very handsome one. Whatever the motivation, it was as a result
of this introduction that the Red Priest was to receive a commission for his
next successful opera, *Ercole sul Termodonte*, in 1723, along with further
commissions – *Il Giustino* and *La Virtu Trionfante* – for the 1724 Carnival
season. And so, in the Eternal City, Vivaldi was taken up and admired by a
Roman society that appeared to be pleasingly free of the class-consciousness
of *La Serenissima*. He was to meet princes and cardinals and to receive the
patronage of the music-loving Venetian exile Cardinal Pietro Ottoboni,
scion of a noble family and earlier patron of Arcangelo Corelli, among
others. Vivaldi, never one to hide his light under a bushel, was also given
to boasting that the pope himself had asked him – twice – to play, and had
been very complimentary. After his departure from Rome, he sent a flowery
thank-you letter to the Princess Maria Livia Spinola Borghese: "I lay at the
feet of your highest grace my deepest respect and inform you of my happy
arrival in Venice, where nothing plagues me except the grief to be no longer
in the service of your Grace," he wrote, further begging to be allowed to lie
at the feet of all the members of her illustrious house.

Vivaldi's fame was now spreading throughout Europe, thanks to his
growing reputation in Italy and to the marketing efforts of his publisher.
Nowhere was he more popular than in France, where the vogue for
his music that arose around 1715 and lasted until the mid-eighteenth

century resulted in the Venetian more or less eclipsing Corelli, previously the favourite of the French. The French were particularly enamoured of Vivaldi's Opus 8, the enormously popular collection of concertos entitled *Il Cimento dell'Armonia e dell'Invenzione*. Following its first performance in France in 1728, the Parisians took *The Four Seasons*, in particular, to their hearts. One can imagine that the pastoral images that this most visual of concertos conjures up would appeal to the French, with their nostalgia for an idealized age of nymphs, shepherds, and happy peasants frolicking in the countryside. By 1729 *La Primavera* – "Spring" – had become an all-time favourite, the young King Louis XV himself requesting an additional performance at Versailles in 1730.

For years, successive French ambassadors to Venice had put on lavish entertainments to celebrate important events taking place in France. Vivaldi, his reputation now well established, was commissioned in 1725 to write a *Gloria* for the occasion of the wedding of Louis XV to Maria Lesczinska. Knowing that Vivaldi had already composed successful serenatas for earlier occasions in Venice and in Brescia, Jacques-Vincent Languet, count of Gergy, French Ambassador to Venice between the years 1721 and 1731, commissioned him in 1726 to compose *La Senna Festeggiante* (The Seine *en fête*), thought to be either in praise of the king

Caricature of Vivaldi, 1773, by Pier Leone Ghezzi.

or as a celebration of his feast day. This large-scale serenata, based on a libretto by Domenico Lalli that depicted figures seeking true happiness and finding it beside the Seine, was a sophisticated work into which Vivaldi put a great deal of effort.

The next commission from the French Ambassador was for a *Te Deum* and Serenade in celebration of the birth of the king's twin daughters in 1727. The French Embassy in Venice had for years been the scene of splendid parties, and this was to be another spectacle on a grand scale. The exterior of the *palazzo* was lit up and embellished with lavish decorations that included Greek columns, with the signs of the Zodiac portraying Gemini – the twins – in pride of place. A huge stage supported by a flotilla of boats was set up on the lagoon for the performers. Guests were able to enjoy the celebrations from the embassy gardens while the uninvited watched from boats out on the waters. Despite the success of this occasion, and, who knows, perhaps slightly to Vivaldi's chagrin, Albinoni was chosen by the ambassador to provide the music for the celebration of the birth of the dauphin two years later.

Although his works had become celebrated in France, there is no record of Vivaldi actually having visited Paris, although it is possible that he might have made the journey in 1725 for the first performance of his *Gloria*, it being his habit whenever possible to attend and/or conduct or even play on such occasions. As well as spending time in Rome, however, between the years 1725 and 1728 Vivaldi also premiered eight operas in Venice and Florence. The Abbé Conti remarked that in 1727 the Red Priest had composed two operas for Venice and one for Florence – *Ipermestra* – in the space just of three months, in the process "earning himself a great deal of money".

Pier Leone Ghezzi's caricature dated 1723 gives us a glimpse of Vivaldi's appearance during these busy years. The curls, the eager expression, and the over-long nose that hints at a need to keep a finger in every pie give us a considerably more accurate insight into the character of the man than the impression afforded by the pair of somewhat bland portraits – the only others that are known to exist – that omit any sign of the fiery temperament of the sitter. Of these, James Caldwell's engraving depicts a cherubic and bewigged Red Priest in romantically casual attire, holding a violin in one hand and a quill pen in the other, while François Morellon de la Cave places his subject in front of a writing desk, manuscript in hand, gazing quizzically at the viewer. The latter portrait, which appears to present Vivaldi as a relatively young man, surprisingly dates from a couple of years after the Ghezzi sketch.

Vivaldi's contract with the Pietà had been renewed during his period in Rome. The board of governors, who had appointed two cello masters

This portrait of Vivaldi is thought to be by James Caldwell. Although generally regarded as the classic picture of the Red Priest, some question its authenticity.

in his absence, had come to the realization that neither of them had Vivaldi's reputation nor his facility in composition. In 1723 he is on record as having supplied two concertos to celebrate the Feast of the Visitation of the Virgin Mary. Subsequently he was requested by the board to provide a further two concertos each month (the postage to be at his own expense when absent from Venice) and to direct three or four rehearsals when actually in the Republic. In view of his increasingly heavy schedule, however, it seems unlikely that he could have met this demand in full. In fact, entries in his name in the accounts of the *ospedale* are sparse during the years 1724 and 1725, after which there is a gap until 1735. It has been suggested that during part of those lost years he may have been incapacitated by illness, although it would seem more than likely that he was totally absorbed by his travels and the many other demands on his time. It was, however, during this action-packed period that he managed to find the time to start on his masterpiece – *Il Cimento dell'Armonia e dell'Invenzione*, which would be published in 1725. It is likely that some of the inspiration for the concertos that go to make up The Four Seasons sprang from his journeys through the countryside surrounding the city of Mantua and on his travels to Florence and Rome, for a man who

had spent his youth among the streets and canals of Venice would have had scant insight into the way of life of the rustic peasants.

The Red Priest was accompanied on many, if not all, of his journeys by his father, to help with the travel arrangements, with general advice, and with the copying of scores. It is likely that Paolina would also have gone along in order to take control of domestic matters and to tend to Antonio when he was badly affected by his chest pains – lengthy travel by horse-drawn coach along the bumpy roads being exhausting for a man in his somewhat parlous state of health. No doubt his young protégée Anna came too, initially to continue her music lessons with the maestro. However, she was growing up, and her voice was developing sufficiently for her to make her debut independently on the Venetian stage in Albinoni's *Laodicea* in 1724, while in 1730 she appeared at the Sant'Angelo in Johann Adolph Hasse's opera *Dalisa* – indications that she was not exclusively dependent upon her mentor. Thereafter, however, it was Vivaldi who seems to have masterminded her career, directing her appearance in so many of his own operas that

Farmland on the outskirts of
Mantua, showing some of the
countryside that may have inspired
Vivaldi's The Four Seasons.

she had little time to accept roles elsewhere. He was later to claim to the
Marquis Bentivoglio that "putting on an opera without La Giro is not
possible". Whatever else she was or wasn't, it is obvious that musically
she had become his muse.

Chapter 13
HEIGHTS OF SUCCESS

Vivaldi's reputation throughout Europe had by now became such that he was in constant demand, receiving commissions from European royalty and nobles, as a result of which he continued to travel widely.

He was back in Venice during the Carnival seasons of 1726, 1727, and 1728, again taking the helm at the Teatro Sant'Angelo, where he would stage four of his operas, in three of which Anna Giro was to star – *Orlando*, *Farnace*, and *Rosilena ed Oronto*. During this period, Vivaldi wrote three further operas for the San Pergola in Florence, in the third of which – *L'Atenaide* (with libretto by Zeno) – Anna was to make her Florentine debut in 1729; she performed well enough, although the opera itself was deemed a flop.

In 1727, the entourage travelled to Vienna in connection with Vivaldi's Opus 9. This set of twelve concertos entitled *La Cetra* (The Lyre) was dedicated to the Emperor Charles VI, whom the composer addressed as "Sacra, Cesarea, Cattolica, Real Maesta di Carol VI Imperadore". The dedication obviously pleased the emperor, and the next year Vivaldi was to meet him during a visit to Trieste, on which occasion they got on extraordinarily well. A talented musician himself, the emperor showered the Red Priest with money and gifts, including a gold medallion, and also bestowed on him the title of knight. Indeed, such was their rapport that Charles, according to the Abbé Conti, "conversed for a long time with Vivaldi on the subject of music; they say he talked longer to him alone in fifteen days than he had talked to his ministers in two years". Subsequently, Vivaldi dedicated to the emperor a new set of violin concertos, which he presented in manuscript to his patron. Confusingly, these were also entitled *La Cetra*, although only one of the concertos had appeared in Opus 9 of the same title. Whether or

An eighteenth-century portrait
of King Charles VI, Holy
Roman Emperor and Archduke
of Austria, by Martin Mytens
the Younger.

not the two men met again is not clear; certainly we hear no more of the emperor until Vivaldi moved to Vienna at the end of his life.

Back in Venice in 1729, the Red Priest acquired a new flautist pupil: the young Carl Ludwig Friedrich, half-brother to the duke of Mecklenburg-Strelitz. The young man, who was undertaking a grand tour, wrote home saying that he had started to study music with the famous Vivaldi. Some of Vivaldi's brief letters to his pupil remain, couched in the usual obsequious language that he reserved for any members of the nobility whom he thought might help to further his career. He wrote in one: '"Since the honour Y.S.H. [Your Serene Highness] favoured me with was like a passing shadow, I must search for something else to console me," and concluded: "My most kind Lord, I implore you never to deprive me of your Protection and to believe me that I shall never forget a Prince who has so many qualities and merits."

Between the years 1724 and 1734, a Venetian opera company staged fifty-seven operas in the theatre of Count Franz Anton von Sporck in Prague. Some of Vivaldi's arias were already included in the company's repertoire, thereby creating a ready-made audience for the composer himself when he arrived in the city in 1729. Here he was to present a revival of his opera *Farnace*, premiere two new works, write his opera *Argippo* (libretto by Lalli), and compose a number of arias. As well as opera, Vivaldi's sacred music was also becoming known in Bohemia.

Records show that Giovanni Battista Vivaldi was still travelling as part of his son's entourage. By then probably in his seventies, he is recorded as having petitioned for a year's leave from Venice "to accompany a son to Germany" – there being little difference at that time in people's minds between Germany, Austria, and Bohemia. In view of the absence of entries concerning the Red Priest at the Pietà between 1729 and 1731, he was presumably once again either ill or travelling abroad. The year 1731 saw him briefly back in Venice, but in 1732 he was off again, this time heading for Mantua and Verona. The trip to Mantua saw the performance of his opera *Semiramide*, followed by the presentation of *La Fida Ninfa* in Verona.

From this time onwards, Vivaldi was to concentrate his energies almost entirely on writing music for opera, publishing no further instrumental collections. Any instrumental music that he did write was either for the Pietà or for private individuals. To these private customers the canny priest would sell his compositions – expensively – in manuscript form. In 1733, for example, the English traveller Edward Holdsworth, who was visiting Venice, was commissioned by his friend Charles Jennens to purchase some of Vivaldi's concertos. Holdsworth wrote to Jennens to say that he "had this day some discourse with your friend Vivaldi", who had informed him that he was publishing no more concertos as he was able to earn more by selling his handwritten compositions. However, in view of the exorbitant cost – a guinea apiece – Holdsworth continued: "I am sure I shall not venture to choose for you at that price." He went on to state that he had already been forewarned of Vivaldi's reputation as far as sales of his compositions were concerned.

A further example of Vivaldi's somewhat questionable transactions is in connection with the purchase of a harpsichord for Anna Giro in 1725. The duke of Massa, having fallen under the young singer's spell during Carnival that year, generously offered her 60 *zecchini* for this purpose. Vivaldi was able to find and organize the purchase of a suitable instrument for the sum of 30 *zecchini*. Hearing this, the duke accused Vivaldi of pocketing the rest of the money. Vivaldi angrily denied the accusation and through his defence lawyer insisted that the 60 *zecchini* had not actually been given to Anna Giro, that the instrument had been purchased by a middleman, and that he himself had had nothing to do with handling any money. As the case was dropped, it would seem there was no substance in the accusation, but the affair drew attention once again to the connection between the priest and the singer that would be to his disadvantage a few years later.

Over the next four years, Vivaldi appears to have spent a fair amount of his time in Venice. Certainly he was there in 1733 and 1734, when three of his operas – *Montezuma* (in which the conflict between the Aztec ruler and the Conquistador Hernando Cortez was dramatized by Girolamo Alvise Giusti), *L'Olimpiade*, and *Dorilla in Tempe* (libretti by Metastasio and Lucchini respectively) – were performed at the Sant'Angelo. In 1734 he was additionally involved in putting together a season of opera in Verona under the aegis of Count Rambaldo Rambaldi of the Veronese Academia Philarmonica. With ominous shades of things to come two years later in Ferrara, responsibility for the engagement of singers was passed by Rambaldi to one Count Pepoli, whose family had taken against Vivaldi as a result of an obscure dispute in connection with Anna Giro. Fortunately, on this occasion matters were satisfactorily resolved and the castrato Pietro Morigi was engaged to perform in all the season's operas, though not without a degree of haggling over his fee.

Back in Venice in 1735, Vivaldi's contract as *maestro de concerti* was again renewed by the board of the Pietà, though accompanied by the rather tetchy comment that he should have "no idea of leaving any more as has been his practice in past years" – a vain hope indeed. For the payment of 100 ducats a year his duties were to include supplying an unspecified number of concertos and teaching the *figlie di coro* to perform them.

In that same year, the young librettist Carlo Goldoni records a meeting that amusingly demonstrates the excitable nature of the Abbé Vivaldi. Goldoni was sent to Vivaldi to arrange some alterations to passages in his opera *La Griselda*, in order to suit the demands of the singer – in this case none other than Anna Giro, who had requested an aria in which she could express passion rather than pathos. The priest, with his breviary in his hand, received Goldoni coldly after making the sign of the cross. Having located the libretto following an agitated search, Vivaldi claimed that he needed to keep it himself in order to finish the recitatives. Clearly, he was reluctant to hand it over to a young whippersnapper whom he regarded as a mere novice. Goldoni, however, politely insisted that he could make the changes there and then, immediately sitting down with pen and paper. Vivaldi began to pace up and down, clasping his breviary and muttering non-stop psalms and hymns in an ostentatious manner. When, after no more than a quarter of an hour of this, Goldoni had completed his work, Vivaldi read it – and his surliness instantly evaporated. Throwing down the breviary, he embraced the young man with delight, then rushed to fetch Anna and her sister, waving the papers and shouting excitedly: "He's done it. He did it here!" Following this somewhat inauspicious start to their relationship, Goldoni could do no wrong; the two men remained firm friends, later that year collaborating on the opera *Aristide*.

In passing, it is interesting to note that on this occasion, at least, Anna and Paolina were clearly on hand in the Red Priest's house – which, of course, if Paolina was acting as his nurse, housekeeper and amanuensis,

A smiling statue of librettist Carlo Goldoni. Campo San Bartolomeo, San Marco.

would hardly have been surprising, though it does little to back up Vivaldi's insistence that they lived in a house *far away*.

As can be seen from the above encounter, age had done nothing to dim Vivaldi's fiery nature, nor had it altered his mercurial moods. At fifty-seven years old he was at the height of his powers, as unpredictable, stubborn, abrupt, tactless, impatient, yet fiery and passionate as ever about what really mattered to him – his music.

AUTUMN

Chapter 14

FALLING LEAVES

CHANGING TIMES

To what extent Vivaldi was affected by the external conflicts of the latter part of the seventeenth and early eighteenth centuries one cannot be sure, but it is likely that he, along with the majority of the population of Venice, carried on much as usual with their everyday lives. During the young man's first twenty-two years, until he was well on the way to completing his training as a priest, peace had more or less prevailed in the Venetian Republic. When in 1700 the Spanish Wars of Succession broke out in Europe, involving France, Spain, Austria, and England in a round of bargaining over any of the Italian states that were up for grabs, Venice had managed to maintain her neutrality. In fact, despite her economic decline and the ongoing skirmishes at sea against the Turks, *La Serenissima* continued blithely enjoying the way of life to which she had long been accustomed, closing her eyes to the storms that were blowing up on the horizon.

In 1714, however, the year in which Vivaldi was to publish *La Stravaganza* and present his first opera in Venice, the Turks declared war in the Peloponnese. This event clearly did impact on the citizens of Venice. Vivaldi's oratorio *Juditha triumphans*, which, as already described, was an allegory based on the triumph of the Venetians over the Turks, received its first performance in 1716, indicating that the Red Priest was able and willing to come up with a patriotic musical offering when the occasion arose. By the time of the treaty of Passarowitz in 1718, Vivaldi was taking up his post as *maestro da cappella da camera* in Mantua. For one so focused on his musical career, it may be assumed that he would have had little interest in the machinations of the politicians, especially as policymaking in the Venetian Republic remained firmly in the hands of the government.

Vivaldi's oratorio, *Juditha Triumphans*, celebrated the triumph of the Venetians over the Turks.

JUDITHA TRIUMPHANS

DEVICTA HOLOFERNIS BARBARIE

Sacrum Militare Oratorium

HISCE BELLI TEMPORIBUS

A Psalentium Virginum Choro

IN TEMPLO PIETATIS CANENDUM

JACOBI CASSETTI EQ.

METRICE' VOTIS EXPRESSVM.

Piissimis ipsius Orphanodochii PRÆSI-
DENTIBVS ac GUBERNATORIBUS
submisse Dicatum .

MUSICE' EXPRESSUM

Ab Admod. Rev. D.

ANTONIO VIVALDI

VENETIIS , MDCCXVI.

Apud Bartholomæum Occhium, sub signo S. Dominici .
SVPERIORVM TERMISSV.

However, conflicts and battles, either from ancient history or of more recent memory, did inspire the libretti of a number of operas for which music was composed by Vivaldi and his contemporaries.

When he returned to Venice in 1735 after a lengthy period of working largely outside the Republic, Vivaldi was to find that times were no longer what they had been. His health was poor, he was worn out from the years of travelling, and his energies had been dissipated by the demands of his work. His home beckoned like an oasis, and the thought of being back with his gifted pupils at the Pietà must have been a relief after the competitive world of opera. And yet, as ever, he was concerned about his finances – and with reason, for a problem of a different kind was looming. Whereas his operatic style had once been new and exciting, it was now being displaced by the work of a rising generation of young composers. Sensitive to criticism and stubborn as ever, he persisted in the view that what had once been acclaimed did not need changing – a common attitude, but one that did him no favours. Indeed, it is likely that it was this same intractable behaviour that prevented

Mantua, scene of Vivaldi's first encounter with his muse, Anna Giro.

him throughout his life from achieving any of the top jobs in the musical world in Venice, despite his fame and success elsewhere. "A prophet is not without honour save in his own country" would seem to ring especially true of the Red Priest. Charles de Brosses wrote that he was astonished that the composer "was not as esteemed as he deserves in this country where all is fashion and where his works have been heard for a long time". But perhaps that "long time" was part of the problem.

THE FERRARA AFFAIR

Although 1736 appears to have been a quiet time for Vivaldi, the next year was to see the first of his three attempts to mount an operatic season in Ferrara, some 75 miles to the south of Venice. A number of letters from Vivaldi to the Marquis Guido Bentivoglio d'Aragona are still in existence, having been discovered in the Ferrara State Archive towards the end of the nineteenth century. These give a blow-by-blow account of the Red Priest's efforts, which appear to have attracted one major problem after another.

Guido Bentivoglio was a second son and, as such, destined for the church. However, on the death of his elder brother he had been recalled to take over the family estates in Ferrara. Vivaldi had met Bentivoglio during his time in Rome while the latter was studying there, and they had maintained some contact thereafter; indeed, the young man is known to have played the mandolin, and Vivaldi, always with an eye to the main chance where members of the nobility were concerned, is said to have written some pieces especially for him.

Charles de Brosses, French academic, historian, writer, and president of the Dijon parliament, who travelled widely in Italy in the early eighteenth century, and who made a number of comments on the works of Vivaldi.

It was in October 1736 that the Red Priest first wrote to the marquis suggesting that he should mount a season of opera in Ferrara. Bentivoglio responded by saying that the Ferrara opera's impresario, Abbé Bollani, would visit Vivaldi in Venice to discuss the project. The ensuing correspondence between the two men on this matter is of interest, for it comprises some of the few surviving letters in Vivaldi's hand. The extracts quoted below reveal a state of affairs in which the scales appear heavily weighted against the Red Priest – although no doubt matters were exacerbated by his own impatience, hasty temper, and inability to compromise. Initially, however, all went well; Vivaldi reported amassing a team of singers and stated that he would provide two reworked operas for the price of the copying fee only – an unusually generous offer. He would be unable to come to Ferrara himself, he said, due to commitments at the San Cassiano theatre in Venice, but he mentioned that Anna Giro would be singing at Ferrara and that she sent her compliments.

The first letter has been lost but the second, addressed to the marquis, begins in typically obsequious fashion:

The infinitely great kindness of Y.E. [Your Excellency] lets me rest assured that you will never forget your most welcome promises made in Rome and think me always worthy of your esteemed protection. I swear to Y.E. that the appearance of S. Abbate Bollani surprises me as much as it has pleased me. I do not hesitate to thank Y.E. and to minimize the annoyance for you, and also because my poor pen would not suffice to show my dutiful gratitude to you. I really hope that in dealing with the before-mentioned Signor Abbate, Y.E. will know that I have no other design in this enterprise than to demonstrate my humblest esteem and to organize a theatre as it should be. I assure Y.E. that I have formed here such a company which, I trust, will not for years to come have been seen in Carnival time on the stage at Ferrara.

In December, however, the first problems arose. Having agreed that the two operas should be *Ginevra* and *L'Olimpiade*, both of them Vivaldi's own works, Abbé Bollani suddenly demanded changes: *Demetrio* instead of *Ginevra*, and then, later, *Alessandro nell'Indie* in place of *L'Olimpiade*. This involved Vivaldi in extra reshaping and copying costs and left him annoyed that his own two operas had been rejected. He wrote again to the marquis: "Allow me to bring to your most prudent attention this little point which has come to my mind without my telling anybody. The Reverend Ab. Bollani persuaded me forcefully to give him two operas. *La Ginevra* and *L'Olimpiade*, and for both to be provided with recitatives for his company for the miserable price of 6 *zecchini* each." Abbé Bollani's first change of mind – the substitution of *Demetrio* for *Ginevra* – was annoying enough, and Vivaldi continued his letter to his patron thus: "I inform you that I have spent for the copying of the vocal and instrumental parts between *La Ginevra* and *Il Demetrio* 50 lire." He goes on to notify Bentivoglio that there had been yet another command from Bollani, to the effect that "he does not want *L'Olimpiade* any longer, but *L'Alessandro in Indie*." "Can Y.E. imagine", he asks, "that this impresario merits the corrections of four operas instead of two, the redone recitatives, all the services, and on top of it, those expenses? With Y.E.'s generosity, he shall have to reimburse me for all this."

In January 1737 Vivaldi sent off the final act of *Alessandro* and wrote seeking Bentivoglio's help in extracting the money due from

Bollani, complaining that "this gentleman does not know how to be a proper impresario". Bollani's underling, Lanzetti, had already written to Bentivoglio confirming the extra expenses that had arisen on account of Bollani's change of mind, but in a later letter he went back on his word – under pressure from Bollani, perhaps – implying that Vivaldi had forced him into writing the first letter against his will. Bentivoglio's response was distant, stating that he would be happy to see the Giro sisters but that Vivaldi should not put himself out.

Undaunted by the trouble caused by Bollani and looking to the future, Vivaldi wrote in May 1737 from Verona, where his opera *Catone in Utica* (based on another Metastasio libretto) was playing successfully, suggesting that a version with ballets instead of intermezzos would go down well in Ferrara. Bentivoglio coolly congratulated him on his success in Verona but, clearly wishing to steer clear of any further conflict, advised against staging the opera in Ferrara, adding that he would in any case be away in the autumn.

The next contact was in November, when Bentivoglio agreed that Vivaldi, acting as impresario, should bring an opera to Ferrara during the Carnival season. On this occasion the Red Priest's plans to visit were thwarted by the cardinal of Ferrara, Tomaso Ruffo, who refused to allow the priest to enter the city on the grounds of his refusal to say mass, and also on account of his dubious relationship with Anna Giro, who, he stated, would be equally unwelcome as a singer. However much Vivaldi had over the years denied any untoward relationship with his prima donna, the cardinal was clearly on the side of the cynics. This refusal threw the whole project into chaos and involved Vivaldi in a potential financial disaster.

It was at this point that he wrote the self-justifying letter to the marquis quoted earlier, in which he insisted that he was bound by contracts, that he could not find a singer to replace Anna Giro ("It is impossible to give the opera without La Giro, because one can not find a prima donna like her"), and that the opera could not be produced by anyone other than himself ("It is also impossible to do the opera without me, because I will not entrust such a large sum to other hands.") He was also upset by the cardinal's casting of aspersions on the Giro sisters.

What grieves me most [he writes] is that H. Em. [His Eminence] Ruffo puts a stain on these poor women that the world never gave them. For more than fourteen years we have travelled together; we were in many European cities and everywhere their honesty was admired, and one can say that also in Ferrara. Every week they do their devotions, witnesses can swear to this, as one who is sworn to one's faith should do.

He went on to explain that his health was the reason for his inability to say mass, "since I am afflicted by a narrowness in my chest and asthma".

He insists that his behaviour in this respect had not prevented his entry into other cities where his works had been performed, even to the extent of playing twice in the private apartments of the pope in Rome. He also stated that he found it difficult to walk, having to make use of a gondola or coach whenever he wanted to go out, and that he required the assistance of four or five people, making his journeys very expensive. "In short," he concludes, "everything comes from that illness, and those ladies help me so much, because they are familiar with my distress. This truth is known in nearly all of Europe." Finally, he stressed that he had been a maestro at the Pietà for thirty years without scandal, and reiterated his assurance that he never stayed in the same house as the Giro sisters. This latter statement, it has to be said, would seem to be a touch questionable.

To no avail. Bentivoglio wrote that he was unable to persuade Cardinal Ruffo to change his mind. Or was he perhaps unwilling to become further involved? Arguing that the absence of Vivaldi was no reason to cancel the opera, he suggested that its production should be handed over to the impresario Picchi. Vivaldi considered Picchi inept, but had no option but to agree. In January 1739, however, he was again writing to his patron, this time greatly distressed by the appalling reception to his opera *Siroe, Re di Persia*, despite its being based on a libretto by Metastasio – a reception entirely due, he insisted, to its mishandling by others. This debacle, he feared, would ruin his reputation. Everything that had gone wrong, Vivaldi insisted, had been due to the incompetence of Picchi. He wrote to the marquis in plaintive vein:

Excellency, I am desperate, I cannot bear that such an ignoramus makes his fortune on the ruin of my poor name. I humbly beseech you not to forsake me, because I swear to Y.E., if my reputation is at stake I shall take action to defend my honour, for he who takes my honour from me, takes my life. The highest protection of Y.E. is my only solace in that case, and kissing your hand with tearful eyes I remain resigned to my fate.

Bentivoglio, by this time having had more than enough of the complaints of his erstwhile friend and his habit of stirring up dissension, remained silent.

A final trauma in the ill-fated ventures in Ferrara occurred later in 1739. Prevented by Cardinal Ruffo from visiting Ferrara himself, Vivaldi had sent Antonio Mauro, a theatrical painter with whom he had previously worked, to Ferrara in his place, to sign the contracts that had been made with the performers in the last of his operas to be presented there. Mauro, insisting that he was merely acting as a stage designer and not as impresario, asserted that Vivaldi had provided insufficient money for him to pay off all the liabilities and that he had had to pawn his wife's jewellery to cover the costs.

Bitter and angry correspondence ensued, with each man pulling out all the stops in an attempt to blame the other. Vivaldi claimed that Mauro and Picchi had divided up the cake to their own advantage, leaving the performers unpaid, and stated that ingratitude and cheating would not absolve his emissary from his duties. Mauro responded angrily that he would be forced to go to the courts where he would reveal "the tricks you used to cheat me, when I was only carrying out your wishes ... it will be your duty to consider your obligations otherwise it will be my duty to find such means as to convince you and to reveal your trickery and your dealings which neither God nor the world can applaud". Vivaldi responded vigorously by reminding Mauro of all the favours he had done him in the past, and insisting that on his return from Ferrara the painter had "bought expensive furniture and laid in stores of wine and flour". Mauro, meanwhile, stuck stubbornly to his claim that Vivaldi still owed him a "not unimportant sum". Mauro's next step was to write again, stating that "to guard my honour and to honour truth I am forced to present to you, Reverend Don Vivaldi, the

A 1775 illustration by P. A. Martini
for Vivaldi's opera Catone in Utica,
based on Metastasio's libretto.

following extrajudicial document attested by Signor Iseppo Mozoni, notary in Venice". The following day a writ was delivered to Vivaldi's house.

A week later, Vivaldi responded by issuing his own writ against Mauro, accompanied by a long and angry letter in which he expressed disbelief that Mauro could have stooped so low. "What crazy brain", he demanded, "gave you such bad advice to write me such an absurd document?" He reminded Mauro of the times he had helped him when he was merely an impecunious stage painter, and that on the current occasion his aim had been to give the younger man the opportunity to earn some extra money. He ended the letter by advising his opponent that "God sees, God knows, and God judges all and that you, apart from facing the holy judgment of the Serenissima, have to answer to God in everything".

As we follow the unfolding of this drama, it becomes clear that while acting as impresario was desirable in that it gave the composer full command over the presentation of his work – and if successful brought in a good return – it could equally place a heavy burden on a single pair of shoulders. When those shoulders belonged to an ageing man in indifferent health, and when one disaster piled on top of another, as in Ferrara, it was a sign that things were getting out of hand.

There were, however, a few chinks of light among the gathering clouds. The year 1737 saw Vivaldi in Verona for the first performance of his opera *Catone*, a work of which Charles Albert, Elector of Bavaria, remarked that "it did not fail to please". Then, in 1738, while the Ferrara affair was rumbling on, Vivaldi undertook a trip to Amsterdam, where he was well regarded and where he conducted the opening concert in the centenary celebrations of the Schouwburg theatre. Outside his own country, at least, his popularity

remained undimmed. And indeed he was also to receive further acclaim in Venice itself; three of his operas featured at the Sant'Angelo theatre in 1738, two of them pasticcios arranged by Vivaldi – *Armida al Campo d'Egitto* and *Rosmira* – together with one original work – *L'Oracolo in Messenia* (with libretto by Zeno).

In 1740, three of the *ospedali* were required to provide musical entertainments during a state visit to Venice by Prince Frederick Christian, son of Frederick Augustus, king of Poland and Elector of Saxony. The prince had particularly asked to hear the girls of the Pietà, and was treated to a concert "with many instruments" to which Vivaldi contributed a cantata and three concertos. Frederick Christian was particularly taken with the serenata, for which Vivaldi had written a sinfonia, and admired the "brilliant accompaniment" of the orchestral players. As a result of this concert, Vivaldi was honoured and given gifts by the noble visitors. This success was followed by another in the same year: Vivaldi's cantata *Mopso*, rather strangely subtitled *An Eclogue for Fishermen in Five Voices*. It was played before Ferdinand of Prussia, and was to be the Red Priest's last – albeit triumphant – appearance in Venice.

WINTER

Chapter 15
THE LAST DAYS

In July 1739, Benedetto Marcello – he of *Il Teatro alla Moda* notoriety – died, lamenting the fact that all had changed in Venice and that there was no longer "a passion for noble things". The complaint was typical of an old man, and a sentiment very likely shared by Antonio Vivaldi. For as far as the Red Priest was concerned, things – noble or otherwise – had certainly changed. In or around 1736, his father Giovanni Battista had died. Had he been alive, maybe he would have been able to prevent the unpleasantness of the Ferrara affair. Throughout his life, Antonio had sought support from his father, and the old man's death had removed one of the props that had provided him with a degree of stability.

At the same time it had become an undeniable, if unpalatable, fact that the Venetians' musical tastes had changed. Vivaldi's decision to throw himself into opera, which has been described as the most perishable form of music, landed him in a crowded arena where his talents were not unique and where he was up against considerable competition. The move had been made largely, and in retrospect perhaps unwisely, for financial reasons. Goldoni rather unkindly described the Red Priest as a "mediocre composer" as far as opera was concerned; the violinist Giuseppe Tartini pointedly suggested in this respect that everyone should limit themselves to their particular talent. Vivaldi, he claimed, had wanted "to practise both genres". Quantz commented that the Red Priest's operatic works were responsible for the decline in the quality of his later concertos and, as quoted by Michael Talbot, continued: "As a result of too much daily composing, and especially after he began to write operas, he sank into frivolity and caprice both in composition and performance." Mario Rinaldi, one of his twentieth-century biographers, was even more outspoken in his declaration that there was "an abyss" between his concertos and his operas.

It was Vivaldi's virtuosity on the violin and the novelty of his instrumental works that brought him real renown; it is perhaps strange that he did not seek similarly to break new ground when he turned to opera, but that he seemed content to work within the style of his contemporaries. Fausto Torrefranca was to comment in the 1930s that in the musical rivalry between Venice and Naples, Venice led the way as far as instrumental music was concerned, "with Vivaldi taking the lead". It is clear that this was the Venetian's great achievement, and it is his concertos rather than his operas that remain as his lasting memorial. His sacred music, too, has borne the test of time: written with deep religious intensity for the ceremonies at the Pietà and elsewhere, it bears the unique style of *il Prete Rosso* – once again confirming that although Antonio Vivaldi may not have been a conventional priest, his sacred music was a sincere demonstration of his faith.

It was no doubt the effect of his father's death and the decline in his popularity in Venice, despite the final successful fling at the Pietà, that convinced Vivaldi that it was time to get out and start afresh. In view of his ongoing financial concerns, magnified by the disasters at Ferrara and the exchange of unresolved writs, his plans to leave Venice appear to have been kept remarkably quiet. Indeed, it seems that the governors of the Pietà only picked up the fact of his impending departure on the grapevine. So was the Red Priest's surreptitious flight – unannounced and at dead of night perhaps – made in order to escape his creditors as well as to hide his wounded pride? Or did he truly believe that a new life awaited him across the border?

Vienna was his choice. Having been feted by the Emperor Charles VI

during his visit in 1728, Vivaldi was convinced that with the support of his patron, this was the place where he would once again find recognition. He had visited the Austrian town of Graz briefly in the 1739–40 opera season while Anna Giro performed there. No doubt he and the Giro sisters could now see new opportunities opening up for them in Vienna, a capital city steeped in music. It is possible also that he had received some form of invitation or encouragement from the emperor; certainly they had remained in touch, for the Red Priest had continued using the title of *maestro di cappella* to Charles VI in opera libretti for some years.

Before leaving Venice, Vivaldi began selling off his concertos cheaply, an indication that his financial situation was dire. In April 1740, the governors of the Pietà bought twenty concertos for a stingy 70 ducats and offered a

View over Vienna, Austria.
St Stephen's Cathedral is
visible in the distance.

ducat apiece for further works. It is not clear whether the Red Priest was still officially employed, even on a spasmodic basis, at the *ospedale*, but there seems to be a faint air of huffiness about the Pietà records that state that "it is understood that the Reverend Vivaldi is about to leave this city of Venice".

And leave it he did. Unfortunately, he chose the worst possible moment to do so. For he had barely settled himself in Vienna when, in October 1740, his hoped-for patron, Charles VI, died from (it is said) eating a plateful of poisonous mushrooms. Charles was succeeded by the Empress Maria Theresa and her husband Francis, duke of Lorraine. On her accession, the empress was immediately taken up with political problems; the concerns of an ageing composer who had passed his sell-by date were clearly the last thing on her mind. So Vivaldi, far from achieving the new life that he had envisaged, found himself without a patron, out of work, out of funds, and facing the prospect of a freezing winter. The last record of his short spell in Vienna, and a poignant indication of his extreme poverty, is a receipt dated 28 June 1741 for the sale of a number of his compositions to a Venetian nobleman, Antonio Vinciguerra, count of Collato, then living in Moravia.

On 2 August of that same year, the Viennese newspaper reported, among the list of deaths in Vienna, that of "Signor Antonio Vivaldi, secular priest, in the Walleris house, near the Carinthia Gate, aged sixty". The date of death was 28 July 1741. When the news seeped through to Venice, there was a slightly longer report in the *Commemorali Gradenigo*. Referring to the "Abbé D. Antonio Vivaldi, incomparable virtuoso of the violin, known as the Red Priest, much esteemed for his compositions and concertos", it went on to state that he had "earned more than 50,000 ducats in this life, but his disorderly prodigality caused him to die a pauper in Vienna". It has been suggested that the figure quoted was a typographical error, 5,000 ducats being considered rather more likely – though who knows? Vivaldi may have been supporting his parents, his sisters, and the Giros for years, as well as acting in the dicey capacity of impresario.

For the last few months of his life, Vivaldi had lived in rooms in the house of the widow of a saddler. He is said to have died from an "internal inflammation", a diagnosis that leaves us guessing, though it may well have been pneumonia or the asthma that caught up with him in the end – fuelled perhaps by despair at the latest turn of events and the extreme cold of the winter. Such was his poverty that he was buried on the day of his death in the hospital cemetery, with a pauper's peal of bells, just six

THE LAST DAYS

Joseph Haydn (1732–1809), once a choirboy at St Stephen's cathedral in Vienna, is pictured at the piano in this portrait by Johann Zitterer c. 1790.

pall-bearers and six choirboys from St Stephen's Cathedral, the church of the parish in which he died. As for his grave, its site has long been lost and forgotten, if indeed it was ever marked. One rather touching note: among the choirboys at the cathedral at that time was nine-year-old Josef Haydn, who, it is suggested, may have been present at that last goodbye to the man who was to become a giant of the musical world – a nice thought, whether or not it is true.

According to biographer John Booth, Anna Giro wrote in 1737 that she and Vivaldi "had been to a good many European cities together", and, unless she was performing elsewhere, it would seem likely that the Giro sisters were at his bedside when he died. They are said to have returned to Venice after his death, where Anna herself was to die nine years later, in 1750. On hearing of his death, Antonio's sisters took the practical step of ensuring that their brother's furniture was removed from his house in Venice, presumably to avoid the demands of the bailiffs – a further indication of the fact that the Red Priest's finances were in a parlous state and that his flight to Vienna may have been principally to escape his creditors. A sad ending to a life that had once touched the heights.

Chapter 16
OBLIVION

After his lonely death in a foreign country, it was almost as if the Red Priest, whose virtuosity had once been acclaimed throughout Europe, had never existed. The stone dropped into the pond left scarcely a ripple. Antonio Vivaldi does not come over as a man given to easy friendships, and if memories of *il Prete Rosso* lingered in the minds of his contemporaries, it would have been as an excellent violinist, a fiery eccentric, and an unconventional priest. Indeed, if he was remembered at all, it was for his instrumental music alone. His numerous sacred works appeared to die with him, and it was to be many years before their resurrection. As far as opera was concerned, he had been one among many; since operatic tastes began to change and he was no longer around to promote his own works, they sank more or less without trace. This was not an unusual fate, as music of the Medieval, Renaissance, and Baroque eras was essentially of a transient nature. Composers, Vivaldi among them, would not have expected their works to last long beyond their lifetimes; indeed, C. P. E. Bach was said to have been surprised to learn that some of his father's compositions were still being played several years after the old man's death. Much material from those early years remained unpublished, and it was all too easy for works in manuscript form to disappear completely, or to sink into state archives and private collections after the death of their progenitors.

The last few years of the eighteenth century also saw the demise of three of the Venetian *ospedali*. The falling standards of music offered by all four institutions played a large part in their decline. Burney wrote that he had visited the Pietà in 1770 and declared that the performance "did not exceed mediocrity". No longer were the girls directed by brilliant and charismatic teachers, and, as we will see, the Baroque music that had suited the *figlie di*

Napoleon Bonaparte surveying the
field of battle, by Ernest Crofts, 1888.

coro so well had itself had begun to fall out of fashion. The fading glories of
La Serenissima and the decline in her wealth led to the end of funding for
the charitable institutions: the Incurabili closed in 1782, the Mendicanti
in 1796, and the Ospedaletto shortly afterwards. The Pietà lingered on into
the 1800s, described as a mere shadow of its former self.

In 1797 it was the turn of *La Serenissima* herself to breathe her last, as
Venice surrendered to the advancing French army of Napoleon Bonaparte.
Declaring that "I shall have no more Inquisition, no more Senate. I shall be
an Atilla to the State of Venice," Napoleon seized vast quantities of booty,
including the four bronze horses from St Mark's Basilica, and then handed
the Venetian Republic over to the Austrians, who allowed it to crumble and
decay for the next half-century. As Robert Browning was to write, it was the
time "when the kissing had to stop".

Over a hundred years were to pass before Vivaldi would begin to emerge
from the shadows, his name even being omitted from several nineteenth-
century biographies of composers. Throughout this period of obscurity
a number of his works were known to be tucked away in the libraries of
various European cities, without exciting any apparent interest, although
it is on record that a collection of his arias was sung at Covent Garden in
1773. And so, as musical tastes changed over the years, the Red Priest had
few remaining champions. Charles Avison wrote in 1753 that Vivaldi was
"of the lowest class, his compositions only a fit amusement for children",
while in 1903 Sir Hubert Parry, despite admitting that Vivaldi's concertos
were "excellent in form", nevertheless complained that his works were
"devoid of deeper qualities of expression". Vivaldi was not the only one-
time lion of the musical world to suffer this fate; Bach too, as we shall see,
was also to drop below the radar after his death.

PART 2   A SECOND SPRING

Chapter 17
A TIME OF TRANSITION

FROM THE BAROQUE TO THE CLASSICAL

That Vivaldi's concertos, published and unpublished, avoided the ignominious fate of his operas is to a great extent due to Johann Sebastian Bach. At the beginning of his career Bach, who was some seven years younger than Vivaldi, had struggled to gain inspiration and to find his voice in the art of composition. Hearing the praise heaped upon the Red Priest's new violin concertos, he decided to use these as his teacher. Accordingly, he arranged a number of Vivaldi's published concertos for the harpsichord and organ. In the course of this activity he was able to gain both an understanding of the way in which they were constructed and an appreciation of the development and treatment of the ideas contained within them. Transcribing and adapting for the keyboard works that were intended for the violin provided him with the knowledge he sought and freed his imagination from a period of what might be described as "musician's block". It is not entirely clear how many concertos Bach arranged and labelled "after Vivaldi", but it is thought to be somewhere between ten and twenty. Certainly many of Bach's solo works show signs of Vivaldi's influence. While it was Vivaldi and Handel, in particular, who promoted those important features of the High Baroque – the concerto and the concerto grosso – it was Bach who was to bring this development to its peak in his Brandenburg Concertos. Following his spell in Venice for the presentation of his opera *Agrippina*, Handel, too, had studied Vivaldi's solo concerto format; although he was more strongly influenced by Corelli, nevertheless he also clearly absorbed something of the Venetian's unique style.

While it is impossible to define the exact beginning and ending of any particular musical era, nevertheless, by the close of the eighteenth century, Protestant Germany had become established as the centre of a new trend in instrumental music, one that discarded the decorations of the primarily Catholic Italian Baroque in favour of a more classical approach. Excavations at the ancient sites of Pompeii and Herculaneum had been instrumental in reviving a Europe-wide interest in the traditional art forms and virtues of the Roman Empire, while at much the same time the seismic upheaval of the French Revolution put an end to the decadence of the *Ancien Régime*. It was indeed a time of change.

The transition to the Classical period in music, however, was gradual. While Italy had been the main exponent of the Early Baroque, as we have seen, it was the northern German-speaking countries that took up the musical baton. Here Vivaldi's near contemporaries – Johann Sebastian Bach (1685–1750), Georg Philipp Telemann (1681–1767), and George Frederick Handel (1685–1759) – all developed their own styles in the Baroque tradition. Handel was to spend most of his later life based in London, where his work was held in great esteem, while the prolific Telemann remained in Germany with a reputation that was far greater at the time than that of Bach. Bach himself was to die in poverty, and his oeuvre, like that of Vivaldi, virtually disappeared until resuscitated by Mendelssohn in the nineteenth century.

Far left: Portrait of Felix Mendelssohn, by Edward Magnus.

Left: Ludwig van Beethoven, painted by J. W. Mahler in 1815.

It was not until Mendelssohn was inspired to conduct Bach's *St Matthew Passion* in 1829 that interest was reignited in the half-forgotten German composer. In due course this led to the uncovering of Bach's transcriptions of the Red Priest's concertos, and the debt that he owed to Vivaldi was acknowledged – though not by all. Certain German scholars, having adopted a patronizing manner towards Italian music, attempted to minimize Vivaldi's influence on Bach, falsely claiming that the Venetian's concertos were of a later date and thus that Vivaldi had derived his style from that of Bach rather than vice versa. In the late nineteenth century, following the Bach revival, a few original pieces of Vivaldi's music were resurrected, with a view to comparing them with the transcriptions. Needless to say, Vivaldi's versions were said by these same scholars to be superficial and lacking in depth when compared with Bach's more cerebral offerings.

The major German and Austrian composers of the second half of the eighteenth century – Haydn, Mozart, and Beethoven – were to be instrumental in developing the classical form of the symphony and the concerto, the sonata and the string quartet, with a structure that incorporated order, balance, clarity, and a simplicity of melody. So powerful were these developments that, with the exception of the performance of a few choral or ceremonial works, of which Handel's *Messiah* is a prime example, the new style almost completely displaced the Baroque. Musical instruments changed too, in order to meet the new challenges. Woodwinds became more complex; the violin, viola, and cello developed longer and thinner necks and fingerboards; strings were of metal-wound gut; the bow became longer and slightly concave; chin rests were brought in for the violin and viola; and the cello acquired its spike. These changes, along

Pierre-Auguste Renoir's 1882 portrait of Richard Wagner.

with the replacement of the harpsichord by the piano, enabled composers to write on a grander scale, which in turn led to the formation of larger and more professional orchestras.

ROMANTICISM AND THE MODERN STYLE

The Classical period lasted roughly from 1750 (the end of the High Baroque, shortly after Vivaldi's death) until 1820, its influence spreading from Vienna and Salzburg right across Germany and into the rest of Europe. In its turn it was to be followed by the next new concept – Romanticism – which flourished from 1820 until the end of the century, in an era that included Mendelssohn, Schumann, and Brahms. This was a time when political nationalism reared its head, and when individual European states and countries began to assert their national identities – a movement epitomized by the powerful music of Wagner. As writers, poets, and painters began to celebrate the romance of the myths, legends, and literature of their countries' histories, composers such as Chopin, Dvorak, Sibelius, Borodin, and Rimsky-Korsakov based works on traditional folksongs and dances, while Tchaikovsky, Liszt, Mahler, and others took themes from folktales. Another important and fruitful source of inspiration at this time was the world of nature. The music of the Romantic era, then, while built upon Classical foundations, sought in one way or another to expand the structure, employing passion, harmony, and lyricism as a means of emotional expression.

The seismic changes wrought by the Enlightenment movement and the political and industrial revolutions of the eighteenth and nineteenth centuries had one enormously beneficial effect – that of opening the doors of the musical world to a wider audience. No longer was orchestral music primarily for the benefit of richer members of society and for religious celebrations; it became instead an entertainment to be enjoyed by a vast new secular army – that of the rapidly growing middle classes.

The late nineteenth and early twentieth centuries saw musical Romanticism pushed to its limits and beyond. Inspired by the paintings of the Impressionists, Debussy, reacting against "Wagner-mania", was one of the first to break with the tradition of tonality (the use of keys in music) and to develop a technique of instrumental effects not unlike the brushstrokes of the new school of French painters. In Germany, Schoenberg began experimenting with atonality, creating a twelve-tone technique that had a major influence on his pupils, Berg and Webern. Indeed, there was a general feeling that the progression of harmonic melodies had gone far enough; dissonance and irregularity beckoned – reminiscent, perhaps, of the early days of the Baroque.

The increased ease of travel and communication in the twentieth century brought the exotic music of Africa, Asia, and Latin America to Europe. Afro-American jazz and blues became the first distinctive musical art forms to arise in the United States with, for example, George Gershwin blending popular melodies with the jazz idiom, culminating in his *Rhapsody in Blue* and the opera *Porgy and Bess*. The improvisational element in jazz played a part in bringing attention round full circle to the music of the Baroque, where improvisation, even if largely prepared in advance, featured strongly.

Chapter 18
VIVALDI REDISCOVERED

It was against the background of musical developments traced in the previous chapter that in 1905 Arnold Schering, publisher of a monograph on the history of the concerto, began to look at Vivaldi's music in a new light. He had access to a collection of manuscripts stored in the Saxon State Library, and as a result of his study of these works he was to claim that Vivaldi was "as exemplary for the shaping of the violin concerto as Corelli was for that of the sonata".

The discovery of the great body of Vivaldi's musical compositions is a detective story in itself. During the Napoleonic Wars, the court orchestra of Turin had hidden its musical archives before escaping to Sardinia. On its return, the hiding place could not be found, although it was rumoured that the collection was in a monastery – somewhere. It was not until 1926, when the Salesian monks of the Collegio San Carlo in S. Martino, Monferrat, being in desperate need of funds for repairs, offered for sale their large collection of music, that the archive came to light. Dr Alberto Gentili, professor of music history at Turin University and a man who had devoted a great deal of his time to a search for Vivaldi's lost oeuvre, was despatched to examine the hoard. To his delight, among the ninety-seven volumes in the collection he was to find fourteen volumes of manuscripts by Vivaldi. These were mainly autograph scores, including 140 instrumental works, plus cantatas, twelve operas, an oratorio, and sundry bits and pieces. Sourcing funds for the purchase of such a valuable collection was not going to be easy, but Gentili was determined that it should not be split up between professional dealers. He was in due course fortunate in finding a benefactor in the banker Roberto Foà, who purchased the works for the Turin National Library, as a memorial to his young son, Mauro, who had recently died.

A view of the city of Turin, home to the Collezione Mauro Foà e Renzo Giordano.

However, closer study of the manuscripts revealed to Gentili that the search was not yet over. Some of the compositions were incomplete, and there were gaps in the numbering of the volumes. It became clear that parts were missing and that the whole collection had at some stage been randomly split between the heirs of the original owner. Further detective work by Gentili revealed that the full collection had originally been in the possession of the Marchese Giacomo Durazzo, Austrian ambassador to Venice from 1764 to 1784 and previously director and administrator of the Imperial Court theatre and orchestra of Turin. The professor's next step, then, was to trace the descendants of the Durazzo family. The sole surviving member turned out to be a nephew, Giuseppe Maria Durazzo, an elderly man who proved extremely cantankerous and difficult to deal with. It took some considerable time and much tact before Gentili was able to persuade Durazzo even to let him look at the collection. Eventually, after pressure on the old man by his father confessor, Gentili's patience was finally rewarded and he was able to recognize the missing half of the oeuvre. It then required even more ingenuity to induce the owner to sell his share – for a hefty sum – to the Turin Library. That finally agreed, there was one further hurdle – the acquisition of funds for the purchase.

The Biblioteca Nazionale in Turin, where the Turin manuscripts are housed.

BIBLIOTECA NAZIONALE

It was Gentili's meeting with Filippo Giordano, a wealthy industrialist from Turin, that resolved the difficulty. By a tragic coincidence, Giordano had just lost his young son, Renzo. Generously, he produced the funds and the "Collezione Mauro Foà e Renzo Giordano" (also known as the Turin manuscripts) came into being, in memory of the two little boys. How the Marchese Giacomo Durazzo had acquired the collection in the first place is not known, but in view of his connection to Venice it is possible that he bought them from the Pietà. Alternatively, since many of the scores appear to be first drafts that would have been of little use to the *ospedale*, it has been suggested by Michael Talbot that they are more likely to have formed Vivaldi's working stock.

Having located and acquired the collection, however, Gentili was still not out of the woods, for Giuseppe Maria Durazzo's obstinacy continued to delay matters. One of the terms of his agreement to the sale of the collection to the Turin Library had been his insistence that the works should never be published or performed. It was some time before this ban was lifted by the courts, but eventually, in September 1939, Alfredo Casella was able to organize a festival in the shape of a "Vivaldi week" in Sienna. This event included two orchestral concerts, a concert of chamber music, another of sacred music, and a staging of the opera *L'Olimpiade*. Earlier still, during the 1920s the American poet Ezra Pound, who was living in Italy with his violinist mistress Olga Rudge at the time, had also become involved in the Vivaldi revival, and had organized concerts of the composer's works in Rapallo. The outbreak of war brought cultural occasions to a grinding halt, and Vivaldi had to wait until peace had broken out before his rehabilitation could be recommenced. Nevertheless, it was undoubtedly Gentili's detective work that had led to the discovery of the Turin manuscripts that triggered the renaissance of the Red Priest, a renaissance that was to gain momentum once Europe had recovered from the devastation caused by the Second World War.

After the war had ended and Italy had been liberated from the German invasion, attention could once again be paid to the arts. Antonio Fanna, a Venetian admirer of Vivaldi's works, founded the Istituto Italiano Antonio Vivaldi for the purpose of publishing and promoting the rediscovered oeuvre. In 1947 the major Italian music-publishing house Casa Ricordi started bringing out Vivaldi's instrumental works. Four years later, in 1951, the Festival of Britain, held in and around London's newly opened Festival Hall on the south bank of the River Thames, presented a season largely devoted to Vivaldi's music, thereby introducing a whole new audience to the Red Priest of Venice.

Once it was realized that Vivaldi's was a name to be reckoned with, events gathered momentum. The next twenty-five years were to see the publication of two biographies in the 1940s: Mario Rinaldi, Vivaldi's earliest biographer, was the first to catalogue his works, in 1945; and Marc Pincherle followed in 1948 with a more accurate and comprehensive version. Later, in 1968, Antonio Fanna came up with yet another listing. As more material was unearthed in libraries across Europe, the Danish musicologist Peter Ryom produced a further comprehensive catalogue, and it is this version that is in general use today.

Chapter 19
THE REBIRTH OF EARLY MUSIC

The Classical and Romantic movements, however powerful, never entirely eclipsed the music of earlier days. Germany saw a revival of interest in Bach and Handel in the early nineteenth century, stimulated, as we have seen, by Mendelssohn's conducting of Bach's *St Matthew Passion* in Berlin's Singakademie. Despite being presented in a shortened version and using contemporary instruments, this performance nevertheless played a significant part in reintroducing the Baroque genre to a wider public. At much the same time, Samuel Wesley was entertaining Londoners with organ concerts of Bach's preludes and fugues, while Parisians were treated by Alexandre Choron to the delights of Renaissance and Baroque choral music in the 1820s. English choirs, too, continued to be active in the promotion of early choral music. By mid-century, the vogue for "historical" concerts had begun to spread throughout the capitals of Europe.

Was it the "sweetness and gentility" of Early Music that commended it to a public sated with the large-scale symphonies and concertos of the Classical and Romantic composers? Did it provide an antidote to grandeur and nationalism? And how exactly should Early Music be defined?

Nowadays the term is used as a universal blanket to cover the Medieval, Renaissance, and Baroque eras – in other words, anything earlier than Classical. In view of the lack of recording techniques, pre-twentieth-century music tended to have a finite life, for it was not known exactly how it would have sounded. It took the efforts of a number of determined musical historians and musicologists, first to dig deep in order to unearth and study the original sources, and second to interpret from these sources the historically informed, or *authentic*, manner in which the piece should be performed, i.e., without deviating from the intentions of the composer.

There are those who challenge this view, suggesting that a slavish adherence to what appears to have been appropriate in the past in fact destroys the very spirit of creativity of the era, thus rendering the work *inauthentic*. The argument continues.

Of the popularity of Early Music – authentic or otherwise – in the twenty-first century, however, there is no doubt, and its revival is due in no small part to the dedication of a number of twentieth-century musicologists and performers. Arnold Dolmetsch was one of the first. A violinist and music teacher, he arrived in London from France in 1883, where he learned to restore and then to build harpsichords, spinets, clavichords, lutes, and viols. He also cornered the market in recorders, and can take much of the credit for reviving that forgotten instrument to the point where it is today in widespread use in schools, as well as regaining its place in the chamber orchestra. Other early pioneers include the Polish pianist Wanda Landowska. Living in France, she brought the harpsichord back to life, founding in 1927 the École de Musique Ancienne outside Paris, where she taught and inspired her many pupils. In Germany, early organs were repaired and workshops set up to meet a growing demand; Dolmetsch's recorder was copied there and taken up by the German Youth Movement. In the 1930s the Pro Musica Antiqua group toured Europe, playing Early Music on old instruments, while in 1933, Paul Sacher founded the Schola Cantorum Basiliensis in Basel, Switzerland, specializing in early vocal music.

Chapter 20
BACK TO THE BAROQUE

David Munrow, whose research and performances were to inspire future generations in the world of Early Music.

After the wholesale devastation caused by the Second World War, the 1950s began to embrace the small-scale beauty of chamber music. A number of ensembles sprang up to cater for the demand, among them London's Academy of St Martin-in-the-Fields and the New York Sinfonietta. In 1967, David Munrow, a significant figure in the revival, formed the Early Music Consort of London – a small group dedicated to interpreting Medieval and Renaissance music, with Munrow himself playing recorders and a variety of ancient wind instruments. In his short career (he took his own life aged just thirty-three) Munrow wrote, taught, broadcast, recorded, and performed prolifically, becoming an inspiration to future generations in this field.

At the start of the revival, Early Music was played on modern instruments. As a result, performances were often slower and more in the Romantic style than they would have been in the Baroque era. The 1960s stand out as something of a watershed, a time when period instruments or reproductions thereof came strongly back into fashion. This reversion enabled players to follow original techniques and thus to reproduce the crisper, faster, and more dance-like sound of the true Baroque.

The development of the recording industry had a major influence on the appreciation of classical music of every kind; here, however, we will focus on the music of Vivaldi. The discovery of the collection of manuscripts by Dr Alberto Gentili, the promotional activities of Antonio Fanna, the festival organized by Alfredo Caselli, and the generosity of Roberto Foà and Filippo

Nigel Kennedy, whose breathtaking presentation of The Four Seasons did much to popularize Vivaldi's works.

Giordano in funding the Turin manuscripts all combined to raise the Red Priest from obscurity. Bernardino Molinari and the St Cecilia Academy of Rome made the first recording of Vivaldi's Four Seasons in 1942, playing on modern instruments, including a modified piano. Then came violinist Louis Kaufman's version, recorded in America's Carnegie Hall in 1948. More large-scale recordings followed over the next thirty years, including that of the New York Philharmonic with Leonard Bernstein on an amplified harpsichord, and a major orchestral version by the New Philharmonia under Leopold Stokowski in 1967.

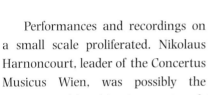
Nicholas Watts (as Oronte)
and Sophie Bevan (as Alinda)
perform in the production of
Vivaldi's opera L'Incoronazione
Di Dario at Garsington, in
Oxfordshire.

Performances and recordings on a small scale proliferated. Nikolaus Harnoncourt, leader of the Concertus Musicus Wien, was possibly the most ground-breaking interpreter of the Baroque at the time. His group performed on period instruments in an authentic style that was vivid and colourful, as demonstrated in their recording of Vivaldi's Four Seasons in 1976. In 1982, Christopher Hogwood's Academy of Ancient Music and Trevor Pinnock's English Consort both recorded The Four Seasons, their interpretations taking a smoother approach. Members of the highly acclaimed Italian group Il Giardino Armonico, founded in 1985, received numerous awards for their startling performances on period instruments, their repertoire including arias from Vivaldi's operas sung by Cecilia Bartoli, and a much-lauded version of The Four Seasons. The year 1989 was to see the virtuoso violinist Nigel Kennedy's take on the same work; played on modern instruments, this striking version became one of the top classical recordings of all time, selling over two million copies. Here was a performance that would have been close to Vivaldi's heart! The British group La Serenissima, formed in 1994 for a performance of La Senna Festeggiante, became another of the leading exponents of the music of Vivaldi and his contemporaries. And in 2005 the maverick group Red Priest, named after the composer himself, recorded their own flamboyantly dramatic arrangement of The Four Seasons and other Vivaldi concertos.

There are now literally hundreds of recordings of Vivaldi's works; concertos for violin, cello, bassoon, oboe, flute, recorder, viola d'amore, lute, and mandolin; there are recordings of his sonatas and sinfonias, his

sacred music, including the *Gloria, Magnificat* and *Stabat Mater*, and the
oratorio *Juditha triumphans*. Early Baroque operas have also begun to make
a tentative comeback, both on stage and as recordings. Although opera was
never one of Vivaldi's most successful genres, those that survive contain
some beautiful arias, many of which have been recorded, notably by Cecilia
Bartoli, as mentioned above, and by Emma Kirkby. Indeed, it was Emma
Kirkby, with her pure "choirboy" voice, who first broke away from the rich
vibrato of the Romantic singer, as a result becoming established as a major
Early Music recording success from the 1970s until the present day.

If he could return, what, one wonders, would Vivaldi make of it all?
He would certainly delight in the money – think of all those royalties! He
would perhaps feel a touch of schadenfreude in seeing how the nobles had
crumbled away along with their *palazzi*, and how his critics and detractors
had sunk without trace, while his own reputation had soared to the
heights. He had always, after all, had a good sense of his own worth. He
would certainly be intrigued to learn of recording techniques, to discover
that people could hear his music around the world at the touch of a button.
How amazing, he would think, that the works conceived through his vital
energy and vivid imagination were still bringing such joy and pleasure!
And then, imagine his return to Venice, city of his birth, to see again the
domes of St Mark's, the gondolas gliding along the canals, the shapes of the
distant islands across the lagoon and the sunlight on the rippling waters!
Inspired, perhaps he would grab a piece of paper and start jotting down
another melody that had just sprung into his mind ...

BACK TO THE BAROQUE

Further Reading

Cohen, Joel, and Herb Snitzer, *Reprise: The Extraordinary Revival of Early Music* (Little, Brown & Co., 1985).

Duggan, Christopher, *A Concise History of Italy* (Cambridge University Press, 1994).
For further reading on the history of Italy from its founding up to the end of the twentieth century:

The Everyman Guide to Venice (Everyman Guides, 1993).
A comprehensive guide, including brief facts on aspects of Venetian history and customs past and present, superbly illustrated with over 2,000 colour pictures.

Haskell, Harry, *The Early Music Revival: A History* (Dover Publications, Inc., 1966).
A comprehensive guide.

McGregor, James H. S., *Venice from the Ground Up* (The Belknap Press of Harvard University Press, 2006).
An illustrated portrait of Venice through the ages.

Morris, Jan, *Venice* (Faber & Faber, 1960).
A panoramic history of Venice, including many unusual and quirky facts.

Mosto, Francesco da, *Francesco's Venice* (Ebury Publishing/Random House, 2004).
A beautifully illustrated introduction to the history of the city of Venice.

Norwich, John Julius, *A History of Venice* (Penguin Books, 1977).
A superbly detailed perspective on Venetian history.

Pincherle, Marc, *Vivaldi: Genius of the Baroque* (Éditions Le Bon Plaisir, 1955; English edition, Victor Gollancz, 1958).
A brief history of Vivaldi's life together with extensive information on his musical style and form, his influence and reputation.

Romijn, Andre, *Hidden Harmonies: The Secret Life of Antonio Vivaldi* (Roman House Publishers, 2008).
A novel loosely based on the life of Vivaldi.

Talbot, Michael, *Vivaldi* (J. M. Dent, 1978).
Vivaldi's life, including details of his musical style and instrumental and vocal music.

Wade-Mathews, Max, and Wendy Thompson, *The Encyclopedia of Music: Instruments of the Orchestra and the Great Composers* (Hermes House, 2003).
A clear and well-illustrated guide to the development of music from the early days to modern times, including sections on Baroque composers and instruments.

Vivaldi's Music

Vivaldi wrote over 60 pieces of church music, much of it vocal. His sacred works included music for masses, three oratorios, numerous cantatas, motets, and settings for hymns and psalms.

He composed around 45 operas – he claimed to have written 93, but this figure is regarded as a wild exaggeration. The scores of a number of his operas have been lost; 23 are held in the National Library of Turin.

The greater part of Vivaldi's music was orchestral, designed to be played by the girls of the Pietà. He wrote between 450 and 500 concertos, including over 250 for violin and strings, as well as concertos for other solo instruments: for example 25 for cello, 39 for bassoon, around 18 for flute, 10 for recorder, 19 for oboe, 8 for viola d'amore, 2 for trumpet, and 2 for horns. He composed for numerous combinations of instruments. A few examples: violin, oboe, recorders, bassoon, and strings; violin, oboe, bassoon, and horns; 2 clarinets, 2 oboes, and strings; harpsichord and strings; lute and 2 violins; and mandolin and strings. In addition to concertos, Vivaldi composed some 75 sonatas, 21 sinfonias, and serenades.

RV numbers, where quoted, relate to Peter Ryom's classification.

Orchestral works

This selection from the composer's concertos (mentioned in the text) was published during his lifetime:

Opus 1 12 trio sonatas (1705)

Opus 2 12 trio sonatas (1709)

Opus 3 *L'Estro Armonico*
    12 concertos (1712)

Opus 4 *La Stravaganza*
    12 concertos (c1713)

Opus 5 6 violin sonatas

Opus 6 6 violin concertos (1717), including the *Cuckoo Concerto*

Opus 7 6 concertos

Opus 8 *Il Cimento dell'Armonia e dell'Invenzione*
    12 concertos (1725), including *Le Quattro Stagioni*, *Il Piacere*, *La Tempesta di Mare*, and *La Caccia*

Opus 9 *La Cetra*
    6 concertos (*c.* 1727) for flute and strings

Opus 10 6 concertos (1728) for *flauto traverso*, including *La Tempesta di Mare* (second version), *La Notte*, and *Il Gardelino*

Opus 11 6 concertos: 5 for violin, 1 for oboe.

Opus 12 6 concertos: 5 for violin, 1 without solo.

Sacred works

Highlights (mentioned in the text) from the composer's church music:

Gloria in D – two versions, of which the second (RV589) is the most popular

Magnificat in G minor (RV610)

Oratorios

Juditha triumphans (RV644)

Psalms

Dixit Dominus (RV594) – setting for Psalm 109

Beatus Vir (RV597) – setting for Psalm 111

Beatus Vir (RV598) – second version

Serenatas

Il Mopso (RV691)

La Senna Festeggiante (RV693)

Stabat Mater in F minor (RV621)

Opera

A list of operas (mentioned in the text), including years of first performance:

1713 *Ottone in Villa* (RV729)

1714 *Orlando Finto Pazzo* (RV727)

1715 *Nerone fatto Cesare* (RV724) (pasticcio, lost)

1716 *Arsilda Regina di Ponto* (RV700)
   La Constanza (RV706)

1717 *L'Incoronazione di Dario* (RV719)

1718 *Scandebeg* (RV732) (lost)
   Armida al campo d'Egitto (RV699) (pasticcio)

1719 *Teuzzone* (RV736)

1719/20 *Tito Manlio* (RV738) (lost)

1720 *La Candace* (RV704) (lost)
   La Verita in Cimento (RV739)

1721 *La Silvia* (RV734) lost

1723 *Ercole sul Termodonte* (RV710) (lost)

1724 *Il Giustino* (RV717)
   La Virtu Trionfante (RV740)

1725 *La Griselda* (RV718)

1726 *Dorilla in Tempe* (RV709)
   Ipermestra (RV722) (lost)
   Siroe, Re di Persia (RV735) (lost)
   Orlando Furioso (RV728)
   Farnace (RV711)

1728 *Rosilena ed Oranto* (RV730) (lost)

1729 *L'Atendaide* (RV702)

1730 *Argippo* (RV697) (lost)

1732 *Semiramide* (RV733) (lost)
   La Fida Ninfa (RV714)

1733 *Montezuma* (RV723) (lost)

1734 *L'Olimpiade* (RV725)

1735 *Aristide* (RV698) (lost)

1736 *Ginevra* (RV716) (lost)

1737 *Catone in Utica* (RV705)

1738 *Rosmira* (RV731) (pasticcio)
   L'Oracolo in Messenia (RV726)

Index

Picture
Acknowledgments

Alamy: pp. 48, 133 Interfoto; p. 80 Derek Harris; p. 93 The London Art Archive; p. 97 Worldwide Picture Library; pp. 107, 166 Lebrecht Music and Arts Photo Library; p. 143 Paul Carstairs; p. 177 Comoglio stock; p. 182 Trinity Mirror / Mirrorpix

The Art Archive: p. 10 Cava dei Tirreni Abbey Salerno/Gianni Dagli Orti; pp. 17, 54 Bibliothèque des Arts Décoratifs Paris/Gianni Dagli Orti; p.18 Bibliothèque de l'Arsenal Paris/Kharbine-Tapabor/Coll. Jean Vigne; p. 20 Naval Historical Museum Venice/ Alfredo Dagli Orti; p. 27 Galleria degli Uffizi Florence/Alfredo Dagli Orti; p. 31 Palazzo dell'Arcivescovado Udine/Gianni Dagli Orti; p. 63 Alfredo Dagli Orti; pp. 100, 103 Ca Rezzonico Museum Venice/Gianni Dagli Orti; p. 134 Museo Bibliografico Musicale Bologna/Alfredo Dagli Orti

The Bridgeman Art Library: p. 62; p. 149 Giraudon

Corbis: p. 135; pp. 2, 113 Arne Hodalic; pp. 7, 168 Christie's Images; pp. 11, 52, 138, 171, 172r, 173 The Art Archive; p. 15 Yann Arthus-Bertrand; p. 28 Philippa Lewis/Edifice; p. 64 Angelo Hornak; p. 76 Paul Hardy; pp. 78, 79 William Manning; p. 81 Andrea Merola/epa; p. 91 Ron Chapple Stock; p. 92 Araldo de Luca; pp. 105, 172l Bettmann; p. 121 Massimo Listri; p. 131 Stephane Frances/Sygma; p. 136 Adam Woolfitt; p. 153 Carmen Redondo; p. 161 Randy M. Ury; p. 162 Fridmar Damm; p. 176 Bo Braennhage; p. 183 Robbie Jack; p. 185 Bob Krist

Lebrecht Music and Arts: pp. 23, 36, 67, 127, 157; pp. 34, 46, 47 Leemage; p. 38 Graham Salter; p. 44 Abigail Lebrecht; p. 85 Lebrecht Authors

Photolibrary: p. 60 Andrea Pistolesi; p. 71 Sergio Pitamitz; pp. 108, 145 De Agostini; p. 147 Wojtek Buss; p. 165 Yadid Levy

Scala: p. 88 © 2000 Photo Scala, Florence – courtesy of the Ministero Beni Att. Culturali; p. 114 © 1997 Photo Scala, Florence

Topfoto: p. 87 Luisa Ricciarini; p. 181 Clive Barda/PAL

Lion Hudson

Commissioning editor: Kate Kirkpatrick

Project editor: Miranda Powell

Designer: Emma DeBanks

Picture researcher: Jenny Ward

Production manager: Kylie Ord